Medieval Gardens
and Culinary Adventures
Stemming from Same

ISBN Paperback: 978-1-989647-12-7

© 2023 R.H.Mason

A Byrd Press Publication
Toronto
www.byrdpress.com
publisher@byrdpress.com

cover design R.H. Mason
All images in this Book were generated with the assistance of AI in 2023.

Medieval Gardens
and Culinary Adventures Stemming from Same

by R.H. Mason

Welcome to the Medieval Garden

In the heart of the medieval world, amidst the towering castles and cobblestone streets, there existed a realm that brought together beauty, sustenance, and culinary artistry in harmony - the medieval garden. These enchanting plots of land were not just oases of tranquility but thriving hubs of culinary exploration, each leaf and petal telling a story of culinary creativity and cultural exchange.

In this Book, we embark on a journey through time, weaving between the ancient and the contemporary, to uncover the secrets, flavors, and culinary marvels of medieval gardens. From the monastic gardens tended by devoted monks to the resplendent courtyards of royal castles, our quest is to unearth the tales of cultivation, innovation, and indulgence that sprouted within these verdant havens.

As we delve into the pages of this book, we will traverse centuries and traverse continents, discovering the delectable treasures that once graced the tables of medieval feasts and continue to tantalize our modern palates. Together, we will pluck herbs, fruits, and flowers from the annals of history and breathe life into their recipes, savoring the timeless flavors that have transcended generations.

But this is not merely a journey into the past. In these pages, you will also find a personal journey as a food historian, student of the and amateur chef who has embraced the wisdom of medieval horticulture and culinary practices. Hopefully, my explorations will illuminate an ancient practice with modern applications, so the echoes of the past reverberate in our kitchens and gardens today, as we rediscover forgotten ingredients, embrace sustainable farming, and celebrate the enduring artistry of gastronomy.

So, dear Reader, join us on this odyssey through time and taste, as we explore the medieval gardens and culinary adventures that continue to shape our understanding of food, culture, and history. In the fragrant petals of a rose, the vibrant hues of a medieval tapestry, and the sizzle of a modern kitchen, the magic of gastronomy awaits, connecting us to an age where gardens were not just cultivated, but cultivated stories.

How to Use this Book

This is a small book.

It began as a series of notes on 4x6" index cards.
Notes on scraps of odd papers. Lists. Endless lists.

The conception was shabby and this collected Book is intentionally reminiscent of that stack of marked-up ephemera and irregular pieces stuffed into a ripped cardboard box.

The result is this brief, practical handbook.

It is intended to provide just enough information for the Reader to plan, plant, care for, and harvest from, a Medieval-themed home garden.

The Contents of this Book are intended to provide the Reader with a toolkit. The Reader can choose design elements, plants and trees that suit their vision and needs.

The Culinary Section is meant to provide a glimpse into traditional Medieval uses for ingredients and a few contemporary approaches to same. It is not meant to be exhaustive. It is meant to be illustrative.

And, finally, the final section of Odds and Ends seeks to provide some aid to enjoying your Garden on a deeper level, either shared with friends and family, or as a portal to deeper communion, peace, engagement
and contemplation.

Final Word:

It might be best to read through this Book, and while you do, plan and think and record with a companion notebook. There are a great many choices to be made, observations to be had and experiments to be undertaken with the guidance within providing the most basic of starting points. The most profound decision is to start this a trek through from antiquity through to tomorrow, using this step as the first step of a decades long discovery,

I wish you the best of luck, and the best results, as you begin your journey into living history. The ideas within have worked for centuries.

I am certain you will find them good company.

Table of Contents

I. Introduction:
Wherein we explore Medieval Gardens, Walled Gardens, and Gardens Around the World between 900-1300 A.D.

- The Medieval Garden   1
- Historical Background   2
- Culinary Uses of Plants in Medieval Gardens   7
- But, were there "Gardeners"?   8

II. Medieval Garden Design, Care and Inspiration
Wherein we discuss the salient features of the Medieval Gardens and explore how the contemporary Gardener can plan, plant, care for and harvest from a contemporary garden based on the Medieval Garden archetype.   10

- Considering the Layout of Medieval Gardens   12
- 10 Reasons to Plant a Home Medieval Garden   14
- Elements of Medieval Garden Design   15
- The High-Level Overview on a Medieval-Inspired Home Garden   16
- Semi-Pro Considerations for a Medieval-Themed Home Garden   18
- Inspiring Words from Marvell and Chaucer   19
- An Inspiring Garden: Medieval Garden, Cahors Cathedral   20

III. Plants in Medieval Gardens
Wherein we explore what flowers, plants, herbs, Fruits and Vegetables were commonly found in Medieval Gardens   22

- Flowers in Medieval Gardens   24
- More Flowers and Flowering Plants   29
- Popular Plants in Medieval Gardens by Country   32
- Culinary Uses of Plants in Medieval Gardens   33
- Medicinal Uses of Fruit   36
- 11 Herbs and Spices Found in Medieval Gardens   39
- Onions: A Special Mention   43
- Fruits and Vegetables in Medieval Gardens   44

IV. Long Pepper
Wherein we rediscover an ancient plant, common to the Medieval Royal tables, and almost unknown today.   54

- Long Pepper: An Essential Import   55
- Medicinal Properties of Long Pepper   59
- Culinary Uses of Long Pepper   60
- How to Use Long Pepper in Today's Kitchen
    with Long Pepper and Lime Cocktail Recipe   62
- The Long Pepper and Sea Salt Molten Chocolate Cake Recipe   65

V. Culinary Adventures

Wherein we use the toolbox of flavours, plant and ingredients and discover historic and contemporary ways to engage with history and the culinary arts, and provide case studies and proven recipes from which to start personal explorations. 66

- Spices and Flavor Profile in the Middle Ages 68
- Practical Examples: Culinary Uses of Plants in Medieval Gardens 70

Recipes

- Cabbage: Medieval Cabbage Soup 72
- Carrots: Medieval Carrot Pudding 73
- Leeks: Medieval Leek Tart 74
- Onions: French Medieval Onion Tart 75
- Onions: English Medieval Onion Tart 76
- Onions: Medieval Onion and Pear Pottage with Medieval-style Biscuits 78
- Peas: French Medieval Pea Soup Recipe 79
- English Medieval Pea Soup Recipe 80
- Beans: Medieval Bean Stew with a Raisins and Walnuts 81
- Medieval Radish Salad, Three Ways 82
- Apples: Spiced Apple and Honey Tart 86
- Apples: Savory Apple Tart with a Medieval Flavor Profile and a Wine Sauce 87
- Pears: Medieval Pear Poached in Hypocras 88
- Renaissance Elixir 90
- Plums: Medieval Plums Roasted in Honey 91
- Cherries: Medieval-Style Honeyed Wine-Stewed Cherries with Rose Water and Sweet Bread 92
- Grapes: Pork in Grapes 94
- Pork in Grapes : *Maiale al Latte* Version 95
- Pork in Grapes : Herbed Garum Pork Version 96
- Simplified Homemade Garum 97
- Figs: Spiced Fig and Honey Compote 98
- Stuffed Figs with Medieval Spices 98
- Olives: Medieval Olive and Fig salad 99
- Quinces: Medieval Spiced Sausages with Quince Paste Sauce on Mashed Sweet Potatoes 100
- Melons: Medieval Flavoured Melon and Anchovy Appetizer 102
- Acorn Squash: Acorn Squash Ice Cream with Medieval Spiced Chocolate Syrup 103
- Orache: Orache Soup with Cream Dollop and Saffron 105
- Medieval-inspired Orache (French Spinach) with Pork Belly and Quail Eggs 107
- Medieval-Inspired Orache (French Spinach) with Lemon and Thyme, and Candied Pecans 108
- French Spinach and Shrimp Terrine with Medieval Flavors 110

VI Medicinal Uses of Plants in Medieval Gardens

Wherein we look at which plants were believed to provide medical benefits and four preparations that may be similar to the plant preparations used by a Medieval herbalist.   112

- Medicinal Uses of Plants in Medieval Gardens   114
- Rosemary Tincture   119
- Lavender Balm   120
- Ginger Tincture   120
- Chamomile Balm   121
- Cinnamon Tincture   121

VII Medlar and Crabapples

Wherein we look at the Medlar tree and fruit from same, why is has disappeared and how the crabapple might be a suitable placement, or a completely new fruit tree to explore for your Garden.   **122**

- The Medlar   124
- The Crabapple as Replacement?   125
- Medlar Tart   130
- Medlar Jelly with Spices   130
- Medlar and Almond Cake   131
- Medlar and Honey Glazed Ham   132
- Medlar and Rosemary Roasted Vegetables   132
- Growing the Medlar   133
- Spiced Apple Cider   135
- Savory Crabapple and Pork Stew with Contemporary Vegetarian Options   136
- Crabapple Tansy   137
- Crabapple Milk Cake   138
- Crabapple Sorbet   139

VIII Medieval Grains

Wherein we take a very cursory glance at Medieval Grains and provide some fun recipes for same.   140

- Cereals   142
- Medieval Oat & Beer Bread   143
- Medieval Honey & Applesauce Oat Bread Recipe   144
- Fortified Barley Bread   145
- Posh Porridge Recipe with Medieval Spice, Fruits and Nuts   146
- Growing Medieval Grains   147

IX Seaweed

Wherein we add dulse and nori to our pantries.   150

- Seaweed Stew   154
- Seaweed and Sea Salt Spice Blend   155

X Honey and Mead
Wherein we contemplate the bee and the gifts of bees.   156

- Overview   156
- Three Books on Bees   158
- Bee-friendly Plants   158
- Planting a Bee-Friendly Garden   159
- Oozy Honey Treacle Pie   160
- Making Mead at Home   161
- Meaded Bread Pudding with Currants   163

XI Saffron
Wherein we mention Saffron and cook Wild Boar.   164

- Roasted Wild Boar with Saffron   166
- Three Side Dishes for Wild Boar   168

XII Two Elaborate Digestif Recipes to End the Food and Drink Section of the Book
Wherein we play contemporary mixologist after digging so deeply into history and experimenting with so many new and odd ingredients and flavour combinations that we should be able to Enjoy a Drink.   **170**

- Saffron and Honey Old Fashioned with Aged Rum and Saffron Salt Rim   170
- Saffron and Honey Liqueur Sour with Yellow Chartreuse Cocktail   171

XIII Final Words on the Medieval Garden
Wherein we wrap up some of the majour themes and present some resources for further study and edification.   172

- The Influence of Medieval Gardens   173
- The Influence of Medieval Cuisine   175
- Examples of Medieval-Influenced Gardens   177
- Final Thoughts on Medieval Gardens   178

§

XIV Further Reading   180

XV. Places to Visit   182

XVI. Other Resources   183

XVII. Odds and Ends   184

XVIII. Three Medieval Prayers   196

I

Introduction to the Medieval Garden

Medieval gardens differed from gardens in other time periods in several ways.

The key differences include:

Ornamental gardens:
Medieval gardens were not just about growing food and medicinal herbs. They were also intended for lush and frivolous play, and some of the earliest references to ornamental gardens can be found in the circle of crusaders in the 12th and 13th centuries. Illuminations in manuscripts showcase flowery meadows, orchard trees, flower-beds with topiary plants, as well as benches, fountains, trellises, and arbors.

Monastic gardens:
Medieval garden style was dominated by monasteries and manor houses. Herbs were grown for medicine, and gardens were an important food source. Monastic gardens were highly praised for their beauty, as well as usefulness. Gardening became less utilitarian and developed a stronger decorative trend in the second half of the 11th century.

Focus on food production:
During the early periods of the Middle Ages, European gardens were rather utilitarian and focused on food production. It was not until the beginning of the High Middle Ages where gardens began to diversify and adopted ornamental landscape practices.

Water features:
Water features were an important element of medieval gardens. Fountains, pools, and waterfalls were used to create a sense of tranquility and beauty. The other two important elements of the gardens were water and shade.

Enclosed gardens:
Medieval gardens were often enclosed by hedges, fences, or walls. The walls had an initiatory and sacred connotation, and the garden became a borderland between two worlds, nature and culture.

Medieval gardens were an essential part of life in Europe from the 5th to the 15th century. I mainly focused on the time period from 900-1300 A.D.

These gardens were not only beautiful, but they also served a practical purpose. They were a vital source of food, flavorings, and medicine for nobility, peasants, and everyone in between. The plants grown in these gardens were divided into three categories: culinary, medicinal, and household use. In this article, we will explore the culinary uses of plants in medieval gardens.

Historical Background

A medieval garden was a garden that was designed and cultivated during the medieval period, which lasted from the 5th to the 15th century. These gardens were typically enclosed by walls or fences and were divided into distinct sections, such as one for edible plants, one for medicinal plants, and one for ornamental plants. Medieval gardens were found throughout Europe, including in England, France, Italy, and Spain.

Timeline of Medieval Gardens
- 5th to 15th century: Medieval period
- 12th and 13th centuries: Crusaders experience garden culture in the Middle East and Sicily and Andalusia
- Late 13th to early 14th centuries: Close connection between several French and British elite centers and the gardens in Palermo

Countries with Medieval Gardens
- England
- France
- Italy
- Spain

Historic Examples of Medieval Gardens
- Cloister garden next to the Dom church in Utrecht, Netherlands
- Abbey Saint Germain des Prés in Paris, France
- Medieval garden, Cahors Cathedral, Lot, France
- French medieval castle garden full of herbs, fruit, and flowers

Famous Medieval Gardens
- The Garden of the Alhambra in Granada, Spain
- The Garden of the Villa d'Este in Tivoli, Italy
- The Garden of the Villa Lante in Bagnaia, Italy
- The Garden of the Château de Villandry in Villandry, France

The Quintessential Medieval Gardener
Sir Frank Crisp: A lawyer by profession, he was a great gardening enthusiast. He paid for and developed some special gardens of his own. His greatest historically relevant contribution is his highly detailed, personal account of medieval gardens.

Walled Gardens in History

The first instances of walled gardens in the world date back to ancient times and can be found in various cultures and religions. Here are some examples:

- The Hanging Gardens of Babylon, one of the Seven Wonders of the Ancient World, is one of the earliest recorded examples of walled gardens.

- The traditional design of a walled garden, split into four quarters separated by paths, and a wellhead or pool at the center, dates back to the very earliest gardens of Persia.

- The hortus conclusus or "enclosed garden" of High Medieval Europe was more typically enclosed by hedges or fencing, or the arcades of a cloister; though some protection from weather and effective protection from straying animals was afforded, these were not specifically walled gardens.

- British examples of walled gardens can be found at Alnwick Castle, Castle Bromwich Hall Gardens, Fulham Palace, Goodnestone Park, Luton Hoo, Polesden Lacey, Shugborough Hall, and Trengwainton Garden in England; Bodysgallen Hall in Wales.

- In Persia, the first walled gardens were places of calm and reflection as opposed to places for growing, and religion dictated their design

The Medieval Walled Garden

The medieval walled garden design was influenced by various historic garden design principles. Here are some of the key influences:

- The knot garden, which had begun in medieval times as a practical way to grow herbs and vegetables, was woven into impressively complex gardens in Tudor times.

- The influence of Persian garden design is still felt today, through Islamic traditions and then via Greece, thanks to the impressions made on Greek and Roman architects.

- The medieval period saw the development of self-sufficient gardens, which were enclosed by walls to protect them from animals and to provide privacy.

- The medieval walled garden combined a grassy and shaded pleasure area with a productive area for growing fruits, vegetables, and herbs.

- The medieval walled garden was typically divided into four quarters separated by paths, with a wellhead or pool at the center.

- The medieval walled garden was designed to be symmetrical and self-contained, with the enclosure providing privacy and sanctuary for contemplation.

These influences helped shape the design of the medieval walled garden, which became a popular feature of gardens in Europe during the medieval period.

An Arabic Saying

There is an Arabic saying about paradise being defined as a walled garden. The word "paradise" comes from the Persian word "pairidaezas," which means "walled garden." The concept of a walled garden as paradise is present in various cultures and religions, including Old Iranian, Greek, and Islamic.

In the Qur'an, paradise, or "jannah" in Arabic, is described as a garden, with the highest level being called "firdaus". The enclosure of a paradise garden was fundamental as it was a cultivated space with irrigation, a cared-for area that excluded the wildness outside. The enclosure provided privacy and sanctuary for contemplation.

The Walled Garden: A World Perspective

The idea of a walled garden has influenced the ideals of domestic life in various cultures and regions of the world, including Europe, the UK, the Arabic world, India, and Asia. Here are some ways in which the walled garden has influenced domestic life:

Persia
In Persia, the first walled gardens were places of calm and reflection as opposed to places for growing, and religion dictated their design. This idea of the garden as a place of contemplation and reflection has influenced domestic life in many cultures, where gardens are seen as a place of peace and tranquility.

Europe
In Europe, walled gardens were often used to segregate kitchen gardens from pleasure gardens, allowing gardeners to work without being seen by visitors. This idea of separating work and leisure has influenced domestic life in many cultures, where people often have separate spaces for work and relaxation.

England
In England, many country houses had walled kitchen gardens which were distinct from decorative gardens. These gardens were expected to provide enough produce to feed twelve people, and ranged in size from one acre up to twenty or thirty. This idea of self-sufficiency and sustainability has influenced domestic life in many cultures, where people often grow their own food in home gardens.

India
In India, the style of palaces and gardens became partly Hindu and partly foreign-influenced, with their form relating to the classic Indian townhouse and farmhouse. This blending of different cultural influences has influenced domestic life in many cultures, where people often incorporate elements of different cultures into their homes and gardens.

Asia

In Asia, the influence of Persian garden design is still felt today, through Islamic traditions and then via Greece, thanks to the impressions made on Greek and Roman architects.. This cross-cultural exchange has influenced domestic life in many cultures, where people often incorporate elements of different cultures into their homes and gardens.

Overall, the idea of a walled garden has had a significant impact on domestic life in many cultures, influencing ideas about the garden as a place of peace and tranquility, the separation of work and leisure, self-sufficiency and sustainability, blending of different cultural influences, and cross-cultural exchange.

Medieval Garden Design: A World Perspective

Between 900-1300, the European Middle Ages, Spanish, Arabic, Mediterranean, Indian, and Asian gardens had different styles and features.

Spain

In Spain, during the Moorish Caliphate of Córdoba, there were said to have been 50,000 villas, all of which probably had garden courts. The gardens were probably walled and included water features, trees, and pavilions.

Mediterranean

In the Mediterranean, the earliest surviving detailed garden plan, dating from about 1400 BCE, is of a garden belonging to an Egyptian high court official at Thebes. The garden is laid out with tree-lined avenues, four rectangular ponds containing waterfowl, and two garden pavilions.

India

In India, the style of palaces and gardens became partly Hindu and partly foreign-influenced, with their form relating to the classic Indian townhouse and farmhouse. Indian gardens were often walled and included water features, trees, and pavilions.

Examples from Antiquity

In Asia, Greek and Roman architects designed urban gardens for escapism as well as to entertain. High walls offered privacy and regulated the climate for all-year use. Asian gardens were often walled and included water features, trees, and pavilions.

Europe

In Europe, during the Middle Ages, gardens were functional and included kitchen gardens, infirmary gardens, cemetery orchards, cloister garths, and vineyards. Vegetable and herb gardens helped provide both alimentary and medicinal crops, which could be used to feed or treat the sick.

Gardens were laid out in rectangular plots, with narrow paths between them to facilitate movement. Gardens were surrounded with stonewalls, thick hedging, or fencing, and incorporated trellises and arbors.

During the Middle Ages, gardens were found in various places, including:

Communities:
Kitchen gardens were ubiquitous in the medieval agrarian landscape from Iceland in the north to the Mediterranean coastal societies in the south. Plants might differ, though, catering for different traditions and palates.

Church Grounds:
Monasteries carried on an ancient tradition of garden design and intense horticultural techniques in Europe. Gardens were functional and included kitchen gardens, infirmary gardens, cemetery orchards, cloister garths, and vineyards. Vegetable and herb gardens helped provide both alimentary and medicinal crops, which could be used to feed or treat the sick. Gardens were laid out in rectangular plots, with narrow paths between them to facilitate movement. Gardens were surrounded with stonewalls, thick hedging, or fencing, and incorporated trellises and arbors. Plants to decorate the church were also grown.

Castle Grounds:
Many castles had their own garden and orchard, although most are sadly long gone. The produce of the garden was destined for the table of the castle owner, his family, and also of course for guests.

Homes:
The cultivation of food was extremely important to everyone, whether rich or poor, noble or peasant. Herbs, vegetables, fruit, flowers, and cereals were the essence of medieval life and found their way into every medieval kitchen. The management of medieval gardens was a meticulous task because food was such an important part of life. Vegetables, herbs, fruit, and flowers grew in gardens whilst cereals such as barley, rye, and wheat were farmed in large, open spaces.

Monasteries:
Monasteries carried on an ancient tradition of garden design and intense horticultural techniques in Europe. Gardens were functional and included kitchen gardens, infirmary gardens, cemetery orchards, cloister garths, and vineyards. Vegetable and herb gardens helped provide both alimentary and medicinal crops, which could be used to feed or treat the sick. Gardens were laid out in rectangular plots, with narrow paths between them to facilitate movement. Gardens were surrounded with stonewalls, thick hedging, or fencing, and incorporated trellises and arbors.

Overall, gardens in Spain, the Mediterranean, India, and Asia were often walled and included water features, trees, and pavilions. Gardens in Europe during the Middle Ages were functional and included kitchen gardens, infirmary gardens, cemetery orchards, cloister garths, and vineyards.

Culinary Uses of Plants in Medieval Gardens

Herbs, vegetables, and fruits were all important components of medieval cuisine. They were used to flavor dishes, preserve food, and treat ailments. Some of the most popular plants grown in medieval gardens for culinary purposes include:

1. Herbs

Sage: Used to flavor meat dishes, soups, and stews. Also used to treat sore throats and digestive issues.

Rosemary: Used to flavor meat dishes, bread, and cheese. Also used to treat headaches and improve memory.

Thyme: Used to flavor meat dishes, soups, and stews. Also used to treat respiratory issues and digestive problems.

Parsley: Used to flavor soups, stews, and sauces. Also used to treat kidney and bladder problems.

Mint: Used to flavor drinks, desserts, and sauces. Also used to treat digestive issues and headaches.

2. Vegetables

Onions: Used in soups, stews, and sauces. Also used to treat colds and respiratory issues.

Carrots: Used in soups, stews, and side dishes. Also used to treat digestive issues and improve eyesight.

Cabbage: Used in soups, stews, and side dishes. Also used to treat digestive issues and respiratory problems.

Peas: Used in soups, stews, and side dishes. Also used to treat kidney and bladder problems.

3. Fruits

Apples: Used in desserts, sauces, and drinks. Also used to treat digestive issues and respiratory problems.

Berries: Used in desserts, sauces, and drinks. Also used to treat digestive issues and improve circulation.

Grapes: Used to make wine, vinegar, and sauces. Also used to treat digestive issues and improve circulation.

Medieval gardens were a vital source of food, flavorings, and medicine.

The plants grown in these gardens were divided into three categories: culinary, medicinal, and household use. Herbs, vegetables, and fruits were all important components of medieval cuisine. They were used to flavor dishes, preserve food, and treat ailments.

By exploring the culinary uses of plants in medieval gardens, we can gain a better understanding of the role these gardens played in medieval life.

But, were there "Gardeners"?

Yes, "gardener" was a profession in the Middle Ages. Here are some examples of evidence:

- Kitchen gardens were ubiquitous in the medieval agrarian landscape from Iceland in the north to the Mediterranean coastal societies in the south. Plants might differ, though, catering for different traditions and palates.

- Medieval sources, such as laws, capitularies, polyptychs, and charters, as well as archaeological excavations, attest to the existence of kitchen gardens and the people who tended them.

- In medieval Europe, gardens were functional and included kitchen gardens, infirmary gardens, cemetery orchards, cloister garths, and vineyards. Vegetable and herb gardens helped provide both alimentary and medicinal crops, which could be used to feed or treat the sick. Gardens were surrounded with stonewalls, thick hedging, or fencing, and incorporated trellises and arbors. The management of medieval gardens was a meticulous task because food was such an important part of life.

- In addition to gardeners, there were other professions related to gardening, such as fletchers (arrow makers), who used wood from the garden to make arrows, and dyers, who used plants from the garden to dye cloth.

In terms of who grew food for the common people or for travelers, most of the people living on the manor were peasant farmers or serfs who grew crops for themselves, and either labored for the lord and church or paid rent for their land. Barley and wheat were the most important crops in most European regions; oats and rye were also grown, along with a variety of vegetables and fruits. Oxen and horses were used as draft animals. Sheep were raised for wool and pigs were raised for meat.

II

Medieval Garden Design, Care and Inspiration

In the enchanting world of medieval garden design, every arrangement of flora and every meticulously planned pathway held a deeper purpose and significance. These gardens, whether nestled within castle walls or cultivated by monks in cloistered courtyards, were a testament to the exquisite artistry of the time. They were places of reflection, healing, and inspiration, carefully tended by hands that understood the alchemy of earth, water, and sun.

Something Old and Something New
Want to add a touch of regal charm to your daily life? Planting a Medieval Garden means you are living history. Your garden becomes a living museum, complete with centuries-old plants and captivating stories. Your taste buds deserve a medieval adventure too! Grow aromatic herbs and edible flowers that knights and nobles once relished. Whip up enchanting dishes that'll make you feel like a culinary wizard.

Considering the Layout of Your Medieval Garden

The layout and design of the medieval garden evolved from 900-1300 as gardens became more than just a place of beauty and pleasure. Gardens became a necessity for survival and a place of spiritual reflection and contemplation. Here is an overview of how the layout and design of the medieval garden evolved from 900-1300A.D.:

900-1000

- Gardens were basic necessities for survival, even for the wealthy upper class.
- Gardens were divided into distinct sections, such as one for edible plants, one for medicinal plants, and one for ornamental plants.
- Gardens were enclosed by walls or fences constructed of supple wood from willows, witch hazel, forsythia, plums, or sweet chestnut.
- Gardens were used for growing food, flavorings, and medicine, as well as for spiritual reflection and contemplation.

1000-1200

- Gardens became more ornamental and were used for socializing and entertaining.
- Gardens featured benches, fountains, trellises, and arbours for relaxation and contemplation.
- Gardens were used for spiritual reflection and contemplation, with benches, fountains, trellises, and arbours providing a peaceful environment for reflection.

1200-1300

- Gardens became more elaborate and featured a variety of plants, including herbs, vegetables, fruits, and flowers.
- Gardens were used for education, with children learning about plants and their uses.
- Gardens were used for economic value, with people paying their rent with onions and giving herbs as gifts.
- Gardens were valued for their aesthetic value, with illuminated manuscripts showcasing flowery meadows, orchard trees, flower-beds with topiary plants, as well as benches, fountains, trellises, and arbours.

Gardens became a necessity for survival and a place of spiritual reflection and contemplation. Gardens evolved from being basic necessities for survival to becoming ornamental and elaborate, featuring a variety of plants and being used for education, economic value, and aesthetic value.

The importance of gardens in medieval life cannot be overstated, and their legacy can still be seen in modern gardens today. However you choose to organize your garden there are a number of paths you can take.

Ibn Bassal, A Garden Designer Profile

One remarkable figure in the history of garden design during the medieval ages was Al-Andalusian polymath Ibn Bassal, who lived in what is now modern-day Spain during the 11th century. Ibn Bassal is known for his pioneering work in agricultural and horticultural practices. His treatise, "The Book of Agriculture" (Kitab al-Filaha), was a comprehensive work that included detailed instructions on garden design, cultivation techniques, and plant propagation.

Ibn Bassal's work emphasized the importance of aesthetics in garden design, highlighting the symmetry, organization, and beauty of gardens. He was particularly known for introducing the concept of the "paradise garden" into Islamic garden design. This style featured geometric patterns, fountains, reflecting pools, and lush plantings, often arranged in quadrants to create a sense of harmony and balance. His contributions to garden design not only influenced the development of Islamic gardens in Al-Andalus but also had a lasting impact on European garden design during the medieval and Renaissance periods through interactions between cultures on the Iberian Peninsula.

10 Reasons to Plant a Home Medieval Garden

Medieval gardens were an essential part of life in Europe from the 5th to the 15th century. They were a vital source of food, flavorings, medicine, and pleasure for nobility, peasants, and everyone in between.

Here are 10 reasons for the purpose of medieval gardens:

1. Food: Gardens were a primary source of food for people of all classes. Vegetables, fruits, and herbs were grown in gardens and used in soups, stews, and side dishes.

2. Flavorings: Herbs and spices were grown in gardens and used to flavor dishes and preserve food.

3. Medicine: Medicinal plants were grown in gardens and used to treat ailments and illnesses.

4. Beauty: Gardens were a place of beauty and tranquility, with features such as fountains, statues, and topiary plants.

5. Spiritual Reflection: Gardens were used for spiritual reflection and contemplation, with benches, fountains, trellises, and arbours providing a peaceful environment for reflection.

6. Socializing: Gardens were used for socializing and entertaining, with features such as benches and fountains providing a place for people to gather.

7. Pest Control: Plants such as marigolds and lavender were grown in gardens to repel insects and pests.

8. Education: Gardens were used for education, with children learning about plants and their uses.

9. Economic Value: Gardens were a source of economic value, with people paying their rent with onions and giving herbs as gifts.

10. Aesthetic Value: Gardens were valued for their aesthetic value, with illuminated manuscripts showcasing flowery meadows, orchard trees, flower-beds with topiary plants, as well as benches, fountains, trellises, and arbours.

The importance of gardens in medieval life cannot be overstated, and their legacy can still be seen in modern gardens today.

Elements of Medieval Garden Design

Medieval gardens were an essential part of life in Europe from the 5th to the 15th century. They were a vital source of food, flavorings, medicine, and pleasure for nobility, peasants, and everyone in between. The design of medieval gardens evolved over time, but there were some common elements that were present in most gardens. Here are 10 elements of medieval garden design:

1. **Enclosure:** Most medieval gardens were enclosed by walls or fences constructed of supple wood from willows, witch hazel, forsythia, plums, or sweet chestnut. The enclosure provided privacy, protection from animals, and a sense of seclusion.

2. **Divided into sections:** Gardens were divided into distinct sections, such as one for edible plants, one for medicinal plants, and one for ornamental plants. This allowed for efficient use of space and ensured a steady supply of food and medicine.

3. **Central fountain:** A central fountain was a common feature in medieval gardens. It provided a source of water for plants and a place for people to gather and socialize.

4. **Topiary plants:** Topiary plants were a popular feature in medieval gardens. They were shaped into geometric or fanciful shapes and provided a sense of order and beauty.

5. **Benches:** Benches were placed throughout the garden to provide a place for people to sit and relax. They were often made of stone or wood and were decorated with carvings or inscriptions.

6. **Trellises:** Trellises were used to support climbing plants such as grapes, roses, and ivy. They provided shade and privacy and added to the beauty of the garden.

7. **Arbours:** Arbours were similar to trellises but were covered with vines or other climbing plants to create a shaded walkway. They were often used as a place for people to gather and socialize.

8. **Paths:** Paths were used to connect different parts of the garden and provide a way to move around without damaging the plants. They were often made of gravel or stone and were decorated with mosaics or other designs.

9. **Medicinal plants:** Medicinal plants were an important part of medieval gardens. They were used to treat ailments and illnesses and were often grown in a separate section of the garden.

10. **Ornamental plants:** Ornamental plants such as roses, lilies, and irises were grown for their beauty and fragrance. They were often used to decorate the garden and provide a sense of color and texture.

The High-Level Overview on a Medieval-Inspired Home Garden

Planning, preparing, planting, caring for, fertilizing, watering, and harvesting a medieval themed garden requires careful attention to detail and a lot of hard work. Here are some steps to follow:

Planning

1. Decide on the layout of your garden, taking inspiration from medieval garden designs.

2. Choose the plants you want to grow in your garden, focusing on vegetables, herbs, fruit, and flowers that were commonly grown in medieval times.

3. Research the planting and growing requirements of each plant to ensure they are compatible with your garden's soil and climate.

Preparing

1. Prepare the soil by removing any weeds, rocks, or debris and tilling the soil to a depth of at least 6 inches.

2. Add organic matter, such as compost or manure, to the soil to improve its fertility.

3. Test the soil pH and adjust it if necessary to ensure it is within the optimal range for the plants you want to grow.

Planting

1. Plant your seeds or seedlings according to the planting instructions for each plant.
2. Space your plants appropriately to ensure they have enough room to grow.
3. Water your plants immediately after planting to help them establish their roots.

Caring

1. Water your plants regularly, ensuring they receive enough water to thrive.
2. Fertilize your plants as needed, using organic fertilizers like compost or manure.

3. Mulch around your plants to help retain moisture and suppress weeds.

4. Prune your plants as needed to promote healthy growth and prevent disease.

Harvesting

1. Harvest your plants when they are mature and ready to be picked.

2. Store your harvested plants in a cool, dry place until you are ready to use them.

3. Save seeds from your harvested plants to use in future plantings.

Please note: planning, preparing, planting, caring for, fertilizing, watering, and harvesting a medieval themed garden requires careful attention to detail and a lot of hard work. By following these steps, you can create a beautiful and thriving garden that is inspired by medieval garden designs and features plants that were commonly grown in medieval times.

Semi-Pro Considerations for a Medieval-Themed Home Garden

When planting a medieval themed garden, soil considerations are important to ensure that the plants grow well and thrive. Here are some soil considerations to keep in mind:

Soil Preparation:
Correct management and preparation of the soil was really important for all plants to grow well in medieval gardens. The soil should be well-drained and rich in nutrients.

Soil Amendments:
Medieval gardeners used various soil amendments to improve soil fertility, such as animal manure, compost, and lime. These amendments can still be used today to improve soil quality.

Soil pH:
The pH of the soil is also important to consider when planting a medieval themed garden. Most plants prefer a slightly acidic soil with a pH between 6.0 and 7.0.

Soil Texture:
Soil texture is another important consideration. Medieval gardeners preferred a loamy soil that was easy to work with and provided good drainage.

Crop Rotation:
Crop rotation was practiced in medieval gardens to prevent soil depletion and disease. This practice can still be used today to maintain soil health.

Mulching:
Mulching is another soil consideration that can help to retain moisture and suppress weeds. Medieval gardeners used straw, leaves, and other organic materials for mulching.

Soil considerations are important when planting a medieval themed garden. The soil should be well-drained and rich in nutrients, and soil amendments can be used to improve soil fertility. The pH of the soil, soil texture, crop rotation, and mulching are also important considerations. By keeping these soil considerations in mind, you can create a beautiful and thriving medieval themed garden.

Inspiring Words

Here is a quote from "The Garden" by Andrew Marvell:

> "Meanwhile the mind, from pleasure less,
> Withdraws into its happiness;
> The mind, that ocean where each kind
> Does straight its own resemblance find,
> Yet it creates, transcending these,
> Far other worlds, and other seas;
> Annihilating all that's made
> To a green thought in a green shade."

This quote from "The Garden" by Andrew Marvell describes the tranquility and beauty of a garden. The speaker suggests that the mind can find happiness and create new worlds in the peaceful environment of a garden. The use of imagery, such as "a green thought in a green shade," emphasizes the natural beauty of the garden and its ability to inspire the imagination. Overall, this quote captures the essence of the poem and its celebration of the beauty and tranquility of a garden.

Here are two quotes from "The Romaunt of the Rose" by Geoffrey Chaucer:

> "And in a launde, upon a down,
> There stood a temple of gret renoun;
> To which ther was gret pilgrimage
> For thider wente the worldes sage,
> That thider come to pleyn and preye
> To the goddes that they serve and seye."

This quote from "The Romaunt of the Rose" by Geoffrey Chaucer describes a temple in a garden where people come to pray and worship the gods. The use of imagery, such as "a launde, upon a down," emphasizes the natural beauty of the garden and its ability to inspire spiritual devotion. The poem is a celebration of the beauty and wonder of nature, and is considered one of Chaucer's greatest works. The quote also highlights the importance of gardens in medieval culture, not only as a source of food and medicine, but also as a place of spiritual significance.

> "And in the garden, as I guess,
> Was an arbour, green as grass,
> In which two lovers might sit and chat
> Protected from the heat of the sun like that."

This quote from "The Romance of the Rose" by Geoffrey Chaucer describes a garden with an arbour, a type of shelter made of latticework or branches, where two lovers can sit and chat. The garden is described as a place of beauty and tranquility, where the lovers can escape the heat of the sun and enjoy each other's company. The use of imagery, such as "green as grass," emphasizes the natural beauty of the garden and its ability to inspire romantic feelings. Overall, this quote captures the essence of the poem and its celebration of the beauty and tranquility of a garden as a place of love and romance.

An Inspiring Garden:
Medieval Garden, Cahors Cathedral, Lot, France:
History and Features

The medieval garden at Cahors Cathedral in Lot, France, is a beautiful example of a medieval garden that has been preserved to this day. The garden was originally created in the 12th century and was used as a source of food, medicine, and pleasure for the cathedral's clergy and visitors.

History
The medieval garden at Cahors Cathedral was created in the 12th century and was used by the cathedral's clergy and visitors. The garden was designed to be both beautiful and practical, with sections dedicated to growing herbs, vegetables, and fruits. The garden was also used as a place of meditation and contemplation, with benches and fountains providing a peaceful environment for reflection.

Features
The medieval garden at Cahors Cathedral is divided into several sections, each with its own unique features. These sections include:

1. The Orchard:
The orchard is filled with fruit trees, including apple, pear, and cherry trees. The fruit from these trees was used to make jams, jellies, and other preserves.

2. The Herb Garden:
The herb garden is filled with a variety of herbs, including sage, rosemary, and thyme. These herbs were used to flavor dishes, preserve food, and treat ailments.

3. The Vegetable Garden:
The vegetable garden is filled with a variety of vegetables, including onions, carrots, and cabbage. These vegetables were used in soups, stews, and side dishes.

4. The Flower Garden:
The flower garden is filled with a variety of flowers, including roses, lilies, and daisies. These flowers were used to decorate the cathedral and for medicinal purposes.

The medieval garden at Cahors Cathedral is a beautiful example of a medieval garden that has been preserved to this day. It is a testament to the importance of gardens in medieval life and the role they played in providing food, medicine, and pleasure to people of all classes.

Cahors Cathedral

The medieval garden at Cahors Cathedral is a living testament to centuries of history. Established in the Middle Ages, it has witnessed the passage of time, serving as a place of contemplation for monks and a symbol of cultural preservation. Today, it stands as a living heritage site, connecting us to the past.

During the Hundred Years' War, this garden served as a sanctuary for weary townsfolk, a hidden oasis amidst chaos. Its towering stone walls concealed them, and its enduring beauty whispered tales of resilience and hope even in the darkest of times.

Today, this living heritage site invites visitors to stroll its elegant stone pathways, where each step echoes with the footsteps of history. Lush greenery and fragrant blooms provide a sensory journey back in time, connecting us to the past and reminding us of the enduring power of nature to heal and inspire.

III

Plants in Medieval Gardens

In the heart of medieval Europe, amidst the tapestries of castles and the bustling life of villages, lay gardens that served as vibrant, living storehouses of wisdom and wonder. These were the medieval gardens, cultivated not only for their beauty but also for their practical and profound contributions to daily life.

In this chapter, we open the gates to these extraordinary gardens, exploring the diverse and captivating world of plants that flourished within them.

Flowers in Medieval Gardens

Flowers were an essential part of medieval gardens. They were grown for their beauty, fragrance, and medicinal properties. Flowers were often used in religious ceremonies, as well as in perfumes, cosmetics, and culinary dishes.

In this Section, we will explore some of the most popular flowers in medieval gardens, including their varieties, countries most often found, ideal growing conditions, companion plants, uses, and any folklore about specific plants.

1. Roses
- **Varieties:** *Rosa gallica, Rosa damascena, Rosa alba*
- **Countries most often found:** France, England, Italy
- **Ideal growing conditions:** Full sun, welldrained soil
- **Companion plants:** Lavender, thyme, sage
- **Uses:** Culinary, medicinal, perfumes, cosmetics
- **Folklore:** Roses were associated with the Virgin Mary and were often used in religious ceremonies. They were also believed to have healing properties and were used to treat a variety of ailments, including headaches, stomach issues, and skin conditions.

2. Lilies
- **Varieties:** *Lilium candidum, Lilium martagon, Lilium regale*
- **Countries most often found:** France, England, Italy
- **Ideal growing conditions:** Partial shade, welldrained soil
- **Companion plants:** Roses, lavender, thyme
- **Uses:** Culinary, medicinal, perfumes, cosmetics
- **Folklore:** Lilies were associated with the Virgin Mary and were often used in religious ceremonies. They were also believed to have healing properties and were used to treat a variety of ailments, including fever, headaches, and stomach issues.

3. Irises
- **Varieties:** *Iris germanica, Iris pallida, Iris florentina*
- **Countries most often found:** France, England, Italy
- **Ideal growing conditions:** Full sun to partial shade, welldrained soil
- **Companion plants:** Roses, lavender, thyme
- **Uses:** Culinary, medicinal, perfumes, cosmetics
- **Folklore:** Irises were associated with the Greek goddess Iris and were often used in religious ceremonies. They were also believed to have healing properties and were used to treat a variety of ailments, including skin conditions, coughs, and colds.

4. Daffodils
- **Varieties:** *Narcissus pseudonarcissus, Narcissus poeticus, Narcissus tazetta*

- Countries most often found: England, France
- Ideal growing conditions: Full sun to partial shade, well-drained soil
- Companion plants: Tulips, hyacinths, crocuses
- Uses: Culinary, medicinal, perfumes, cosmetics
- Folklore: Daffodils were associated with the Greek myth of Narcissus and were often used in religious ceremonies. They were also believed to have healing properties and were used to treat a variety of ailments, including respiratory issues and skin conditions.

5. Tulips
- Varieties: *Tulipa sylvestris, Tulipa clusiana, Tulipa gesneriana*
- Countries most often found: Turkey, France, England
- Ideal growing conditions: Full sun, welldrained soil
- Companion plants: Daffodils, hyacinths, crocuses
- Uses: Culinary, medicinal, perfumes, cosmetics
- Folklore: Tulips were associated with the Ottoman Empire and were often used in religious ceremonies. They were also believed to have healing properties and were used to treat a variety of ailments, including fever, headaches, and stomach issues.

6. Hyacinths
- Varieties: *Hyacinthus orientalis, Hyacinthus litwinowii, Hyacinthus transcaspicus*
- Countries most often found: Turkey, France, England
- Ideal growing conditions: Full sun to partial shade, well-drained soil
- Companion plants: Daffodils, tulips, crocuses
- Uses: Culinary, medicinal, perfumes, cosmetics
- Folklore: Hyacinths were associated with the Greek myth of Hyacinthus and were often used in religious ceremonies. They were also believed to have healing properties and were used to treat a variety of ailments, including respiratory issues and skin conditions.

7. Crocuses
- Varieties: *Crocus sativus, Crocus vernus, Crocus chrysanthus*
- Countries most often found: Turkey, France, England
- Ideal growing conditions: Full sun to partial shade, welldrained soil
- Companion plants: Daffodils, tulips, hyacinths
- Uses: Culinary, medicinal, perfumes, cosmetics
- Folklore: Crocuses were associated with the Greek myth of Crocus and were often used in religious ceremonies. They were also believed to have healing properties and were used to treat a variety of ailments, including respiratory issues and skin conditions.

8. Poppies
- Varieties: *Papaver rhoeas, Papaver somniferum, Papaver orientale*
- Countries most often found: England, France, Italy
- Ideal growing conditions: Full sun, well-drained soil
- Companion plants: Lavender, thyme, sage

- **Uses:** Culinary, medicinal, perfumes, cosmetics
- **Folklore:** Poppies were associated with the Greek myth of Demeter and were often used in religious ceremonies. They were also believed to have healing properties and were used to treat a variety of ailments, including pain and insomnia.

9. Columbines
- **Varieties:** *Aquilegia vulgaris, Aquilegia canadensis, Aquilegia chrysantha*
- **Countries most often found:** England, France, Italy
- **Ideal growing conditions:** Partial shade, well-drained soil
- **Companion plants:** Roses, lilies, irises
- **Uses:** Culinary, medicinal, perfumes, cosmetics
- **Folklore:** Columbines were associated with the Virgin Mary and were often used in religious ceremonies. They were also believed to have healing properties and were used to treat a variety of ailments, including fever and digestive issues.

10. Foxgloves
- **Varieties:** *Digitalis purpurea, Digitalis grandiflora, Digitalis lutea*
- **Countries most often found:** England, France, Italy
- **Ideal growing conditions:** Partial shade, welldrained soil
- **Companion plants:** Roses, lilies, irises
- **Uses:** Medicinal, perfumes, cosmetics
- **Folklore:** Foxgloves were associated with the Greek myth of Pan and were often used in religious ceremonies. They were also believed to have healing properties and were used to treat a variety of ailments, including heart conditions.

11. Hollyhocks
- **Varieties:** *Alcea rosea, Alcea rugosa, Alcea ficifolia*
- **Countries most often found:** England, France, Italy
- **Ideal growing conditions:** Full sun, well-drained soil
- **Companion plants:** Roses, lilies, irises
- **Uses:** Culinary, medicinal, perfumes, cosmetics
- **Folklore:** Hollyhocks were associated with the Greek myth of Althaea and were often used in religious ceremonies. They were also believed to have healing properties and were used to treat a variety of ailments, including respiratory issues and skin conditions.

12. Canterbury Bells
- **Varieties:** *Campanula medium*
- **Countries most often found:** England, France, Italy
- **Ideal growing conditions:** Full sun to partial shade, welldrained soil
- **Companion plants:** Roses, lilies, irises
- **Uses:** Ornamental, cut flowers
- **Folklore:** Canterbury Bells were named after the city of Canterbury in England. They were believed to bring good luck and were often used in religious ceremonies.

Rose, Lilly, Iris

Roses were popular in medieval European gardens, and they were often grown for their medicinal properties as well as for ornamental purposes. The oil extracted from roses, known as rosewater, was used in perfumes and cosmetics.

Lilies have strong religious symbolism in various cultures. In Christianity, the lily symbolizes purity and the Virgin Mary. It's often associated with the Annunciation, when the angel Gabriel announced Mary's impending motherhood.

The iris has been used in heraldry as a symbol of power and majesty. It was often incorporated into the coat of arms of royal families and noble houses.

Sweet Myrtle

One charming anecdote about sweet myrtle comes from the tradition of brides in ancient Greece and Rome. Brides would wear wreaths of myrtle in their hair on their wedding day, symbolizing love, fidelity, and the hope for a happy marriage. These myrtle wreaths were often passed down from generation to generation as family heirlooms.

The sweet fragrance of myrtle was believed to bring good fortune and happiness to the newlyweds. After the wedding, the bride would plant the myrtle wreath in her garden as a lasting symbol of their love. If the myrtle thrived and continued to flourish, it was considered an auspicious sign for the marriage.

This tradition beautifully illustrates the deep cultural and symbolic significance of sweet myrtle in celebrating love and commitment in ancient times, making it more than just a fragrant plant but a symbol of enduring devotion and marital bliss.

More Flowers and Flowering Plants for a Medieval-themed Garden

1. **Periwinkles**
   - **Varieties:** *Vinca minor, Vinca major*
   - **Countries most often found:** Europe, North Africa
   - **Ideal growing conditions:** Partial shade to full sun, well-drained soil
   - **Companion plants:** Primroses, daisies, violets, gillyflowers
   - **Uses:** Ornamental, medicinal
   - **Folklore:** Periwinkles were associated with the Greek myth of Persephone and were often used in religious ceremonies. They were also believed to have healing properties and were used to treat a variety of ailments.

2. **Primroses**
   - **Varieties:** *Primula vulgaris, Primula veris, Primula elatior*
   - **Countries most often found:** Europe, Asia
   - **Ideal growing conditions:** Partial shade to full sun, well-drained soil
   - **Companion plants:** Periwinkles, daisies, violets, gillyflowers
   - **Uses:** Ornamental, medicinal
   - **Folklore:** Primroses were associated with the Greek myth of Hermes and were often used in religious ceremonies. They were also believed to have healing properties and were used to treat a variety of ailments.

3. **Violets**
   - **Varieties:** *Viola odorata, Viola cornuta, Viola tricolor*
   - **Countries most often found:** Europe, Asia
   - **Ideal growing conditions:** Partial shade to full sun, well-drained soil
   - **Companion plants:** Periwinkles, primroses, daisies, gillyflowers
   - **Uses:** Ornamental, medicinal
   - **Folklore:** Violets were associated with the Greek myth of Io and were often used in religious ceremonies. They were also believed to have healing properties and were used to treat a variety of ailments.

4. **Gillyflowers**
   - **Varieties:** *Dianthus barbatus, Dianthus caryophyllus, Dianthus deltoides*
   - **Countries most often found:** Europe, Asia
   - **Ideal growing conditions:** Full sun, well-drained soil
   - **Companion plants:** Periwinkles, primroses, violets, daisies
   - **Uses:** Ornamental, medicinal
   - **Folklore:** Gillyflowers were associated with the Greek myth of Adonis and were often used in religious ceremonies. They were also believed to have healing properties and were used to treat a variety of ailments.

5. **Daisies**
   - **Varieties:** *Bellis perennis, Leucanthemum vulgare, Chrysanthemum leucanthemum*

- **Countries most often found:** Europe, Asia
- **Ideal growing conditions:** Full sun to partial shade, well-drained soil
- **Companion plants:** Periwinkles, primroses, violets, gillyflowers
- **Uses:** Ornamental, medicinal
- **Folklore:** Daisies were associated with the Greek myth of Demeter and were often used in religious ceremonies. They were also believed to have healing properties and were used to treat a variety of ailments.

6. Sweet Bay
- **Varieties:** *Laurus nobilis*
- **Countries most often found:** Mediterranean region
- **Ideal growing conditions:** Full sun to partial shade, well-drained soil
- **Companion plants:** Sweet myrtle, rosemary, sage, thyme, winter savory
- **Uses:** Culinary, medicinal
- **Folklore:** Sweet Bay was associated with the Greek god Apollo and was often used in religious ceremonies. It was also believed to have healing properties and was used to treat a variety of ailments.

7. Sweet Myrtle
- **Varieties:** *Myrtus communis*
- **Countries most often found:** Mediterranean region
- **Ideal growing conditions:** Full sun to partial shade, well-drained soil
- **Companion plants:** Sweet bay, rosemary, sage, thyme, winter savory
- **Uses:** Culinary, medicinal
- **Folklore:** Sweet Myrtle was associated with the Greek goddess Aphrodite and was often used in religious ceremonies. It was also believed to have healing properties and was used to treat a variety of ailments.

8. Winter Savory
- **Varieties:** *Satureja montana*, *Satureja hortensis*
- **Countries most often found:** Europe, Asia
- **Ideal growing conditions:** Full sun, well-drained soil
- **Companion plants:** Sweet bay, sweet myrtle, rosemary, sage, thyme
- **Uses:** Culinary, medicinal
- **Folklore:** Winter Savory was associated with the Greek god Zeus and was often used in religious ceremonies. It was also believed to have healing properties and was used to treat a variety of ailments.

9. Calendula
- **Varieties:** *Calendula officinalis*
- **Countries most often found:** Europe, Asia
- **Ideal growing conditions:** Full sun to partial shade, well-drained soil
- **Companion plants:** Marshmallow, primrose, peony, pulmonaria, catmint, cyclamen
- **Uses:** Ornamental, medicinal
- **Folklore:** Calendula was associated with the Greek myth of Clytie and was often used in religious ceremonies. It was also believed to have healing properties and was used to treat a variety of ailments.

Sweet Bay

One fascinating anecdote about sweet bay involves its connection to ancient Greek mythology and the Oracle of Delphi. The Oracle of Delphi, situated in the sanctuary of Apollo, was one of the most famous oracles in the ancient world. People from all over would seek the Oracle's wisdom and guidance.

The priestesses at the Oracle, known as the Pythia, were believed to be able to communicate with the gods. They would sit on a tripod stool over a fissure in the ground, inhale sweet bay fumes, and enter a trance-like state to deliver prophecies and oracles.

The sweet bay leaves played a crucial role in these rituals. They were burned as incense, filling the chamber with a fragrant smoke. It was believed that inhaling the sweet bay fumes helped the Pythia connect with the divine and receive insights into the future. The Oracle of Delphi's pronouncements influenced political decisions, military campaigns, and the course of history in ancient Greece.

Popular Plants in Medieval Gardens by Country

Medieval gardens in different countries featured a variety of popular plants that were grown for food, medicine, and pleasure.

The plants varied depending on the climate, soil, and cultural preferences of each country.

Some of the most popular plants in medieval gardens included roses, lilies, violets, crocuses, pinks, carnations, medicinal herbs, and vegetables. These plants were a testament to the importance of gardens in medieval life and their legacy can still be seen in modern gardens today.

Here is a comprehensive list of popular plants in medieval gardens by country, based on available records:

France:
- Roses
- Lilies
- Violets
- Crocuses
- Pinks
- Carnations
- Medicinal herbs
- Vegetables

Germany:
- White and red roses
- Lilies
- Violets
- Crocuses
- Pinks
- Carnations
- Medicinal herbs
- Vegetables

England:
- Sweet bay (*Laurus nobilis*)
- Sweet myrtle (*Myrtus communis*)
- Rosemary
- Sage
- Thyme
- Winter savory
- Lavender
- Marjoram
- Fennel
- Parsley
- Dill
- Chives
- Mint
- Hyssop
- Chamomile
- Calendula
- Poppies
- Columbines
- Foxgloves
- Hollyhocks
- Canterbury bells
- Sweet peas
- Roses
- Lilies
- Irises
- Daffodils
- Tulips
- Primroses
- Cowslips
- Snowdrops
- Bluebells
- Medicinal herbs

Italy:
- Citrus trees
- Pomegranates
- Figs
- Olives
- Grapes
- Medicinal herbs
- Vegetables

Culinary Uses of Plants in Medieval Gardens

Medieval gardens were not only beautiful, but they also served a practical purpose. They were a vital source of food, flavorings, and medicine for nobility, peasants, and everyone in between. The plants grown in these gardens were divided into three categories: culinary, medicinal, and household use[4]. In this article, we will explore the culinary uses of plants in medieval gardens.

1. Herbs

Herbs were a staple in medieval cuisine. They were used to flavor dishes, preserve food, and treat ailments. Some of the most popular herbs grown in medieval gardens include:

Sage:
Sage was a popular herb in medieval cuisine. It was used to flavor meat dishes, soups, and stews. It was also used to treat sore throats and digestive issues.

Rosemary:
Rosemary was another popular herb in medieval cuisine. It was used to flavor meat dishes, bread, and cheese. It was also used to treat headaches and improve memory.

Thyme:
Thyme was a versatile herb in medieval cuisine. It was used to flavor meat dishes, soups, and stews. It was also used to treat respiratory issues and digestive problems.

Parsley:
Parsley was a popular herb in medieval cuisine. It was used to flavor soups, stews, and sauces. It was also used to treat kidney and bladder problems.

Mint:
Mint was a refreshing herb in medieval cuisine. It was used to flavor drinks, desserts, and sauces. It was also used to treat digestive issues and headaches.

2. Vegetables

Vegetables were an important part of medieval cuisine. They were used in soups, stews, and side dishes. Some of the most popular vegetables grown in medieval gardens include:

Onions:
Onions were a staple in medieval cuisine. They were used in soups, stews, and sauces. They were also used to treat colds and respiratory issues.

Carrots:
Carrots were a popular vegetable in medieval cuisine. They were used in soups, stews, and side dishes. They were also used to treat digestive issues and improve eyesight.

Cabbage:
Cabbage was a versatile vegetable in medieval cuisine. It was used in soups, stews, and side dishes. It was also used to treat digestive issues and respiratory problems

Peas:
Peas were a popular vegetable in medieval cuisine. They were used in soups, stews, and side dishes. They were also used to treat kidney and bladder problems.

3. Fruits

Fruit growing in medieval times had a rich history that evolved over centuries. Fruit cultivation was influenced by the knowledge inherited from ancient civilizations like the Romans and Greeks, but it also adapted to the specific climatic conditions and agricultural practices of the medieval period. Monastic gardens played a significant role in preserving and expanding this knowledge. The medieval period saw the establishment of orchards, where a variety of fruit trees such as apples, pears, plums, and cherries were cultivated. Orchards were meticulously maintained, often using techniques like espalier and pleaching to maximize fruit production within the available space. The knowledge of grafting and propagating fruit trees was also passed down, contributing to the diversity of fruit varieties. Fruit cultivation was not only essential for dietary needs but was also integrated into the aesthetics of gardens, reflecting the broader medieval emphasis on beauty and practicality in the cultivation of both ornamental and edible plants.

Fruits played a pivotal role in medieval cuisine and medicine. They were used in a wide range of dishes, from sweet tarts and pies to savory stews and sauces. Fruits were often included in medieval feasts and banquets, showcasing their significance in medieval culinary culture. In medicine, fruits were valued for their nutritional and medicinal properties. They were used to treat various ailments and were sometimes incorporated into remedies and tonics. Monasteries and herbalists were key sources of knowledge on the medicinal uses of fruits and herbs. Fruits also had symbolic and allegorical meanings in medieval culture and art, often representing themes of love, virtue, and the passage of time. This dual role of fruits in both the kitchen and the apothecary exemplified their multifaceted importance in medieval society.

Fruits were a sweet addition to medieval cuisine. Medieval orchards were integral to sustaining the nutritional needs of people during the Middle Ages. Orchards were carefully tended areas where fruit-bearing trees, primarily apple, pear, and plum trees, were cultivated. These orchards served as a valuable source of fresh fruit, as well as ingredients for various culinary dishes, preserves, and even beverages like cider. Orchards were typically found in monastic gardens, castle estates, and manor houses, and they were meticulously planned and maintained to optimize fruit production. One distinctive technique employed in medieval orchards was the use of "espalier" and "pleached" trees.

Espalier

Espalier is a horticultural technique where fruit trees are pruned and trained to grow flat against a wall, trellis, or support structure in a specific pattern. The term "espalier" is derived from the French word "épauler," which means "to shoulder" or "to support." This method allowed gardeners to save space, optimize sunlight exposure, and facilitate easier maintenance and harvesting of the fruit. Espaliered trees were often trained into intricate designs, making them not only productive but also ornamental features in the garden. Alongside espalier, "pleached" trees were also common, where trees were trained to form archways or living fences, further enhancing the aesthetics and functionality of the orchard. The use of espalier and pleached trees demonstrated the ingenuity and resourcefulness of medieval gardeners in maximizing the utility of their orchards within the limited space and resources available.

Medicinal Uses of Fruit

Medieval fruits were not only a source of food but also a source of medicine. The plants grown in medieval gardens were used for a variety of medicinal purposes, from treating common ailments to more serious illnesses. The 15 fruits listed above were commonly grown in medieval gardens and were used for a variety of medicinal purposes. They can still be grown today and used for their medicinal properties, as well as for their culinary uses.

1. Watermelon
Watermelon was a popular fruit in medieval Europe. It was used to treat heatstroke, fever, and dehydration. Watermelon was grown in warm regions of Europe, such as Spain and Italy.

2. Wild Strawberry
Wild strawberries were a popular fruit in medieval Europe. They were used to treat digestive problems, respiratory infections, and skin conditions. Wild strawberries were grown in many regions of Europe, including England, France, and Germany.

3. Melon
Melons were a popular fruit in medieval Europe. They were used to treat digestive problems, respiratory infections, and fever. Melons were grown in warm regions of Europe, such as Spain and Italy.

4. Blackberry
Blackberries were a popular fruit in medieval Europe. They were used to treat digestive problems, respiratory infections, and skin conditions. Blackberries were grown in many regions of Europe, including England, France, and Germany.

5. Medlar
Medlar was a popular fruit in medieval Europe. It was used to treat digestive problems, respiratory infections, and menstrual cramps. Medlar was grown in many regions of Europe, including England, France, and Germany. It was also a staple of medieval monasteries and royal courtyards.

6. Peach
Peaches were introduced to Europe from Asia in medieval times. They were used to treat digestive problems, respiratory infections, and skin conditions. Peaches were grown in warm regions of Europe, such as Spain and Italy.

Medieval Europeans had access to different varieties of peaches, including both clingstone and freestone varieties. Clingstone peaches have flesh that clings to the stone, while freestone peaches have flesh that easily separates from the stone. The choice of variety would affect how they were used in recipes.

7. Apricot
Apricots were introduced to Europe from Asia in medieval times. They were used to treat digestive problems, respiratory infections, and skin conditions. Apricots were grown in warm regions of Europe, such as Spain and Italy.

8. Cherry
Cherries were introduced to Europe from Asia in medieval times. They were used to treat digestive problems, respiratory infections, and skin conditions. Cherries were grown in many regions of Europe, including England, France, and Germany.

9. Citron
Citron was used in several medications in medieval times. It was grown in warm regions of Europe, such as Spain and Italy. Citron was also used in religious ceremonies and was believed to have purifying properties.

Medieval citron, also known as the "Buddha's Hand," was a prized citrus fruit in Europe. Its fragrant, finger-like segments were used as a symbol of luck and were valued for their aromatic zest in culinary and medicinal preparations.

10. Lemon
Lemons were used in several medications in medieval times. They were grown in warm regions of Europe, such as Spain and Italy. Lemons were also used to treat scurvy, a disease caused by vitamin C deficiency.

11. Orange
Oranges were introduced to Europe from Asia in medieval times. They were used to treat digestive problems, respiratory infections, and skin conditions. Oranges were grown in warm regions of Europe, such as Spain and Italy.

12. Apple
Apples were a popular fruit in medieval Europe. They were used to treat digestive problems, respiratory infections, and skin conditions. Apples were grown in many regions of Europe, including England, France, and Germany.

13. Pear
Pears were a popular fruit in medieval Europe. They were used to treat digestive problems, respiratory infections, and skin conditions. Pears were grown in many regions of Europe, including England, France, and Germany.

14. Quince
Quinces were a popular fruit in medieval Europe. They were used to treat digestive problems, respiratory infections, and skin conditions. Quinces were grown in many regions of Europe, including England, France, and Germany.

15. Grape
Grapes were a popular fruit in medieval Europe. They were used to treat digestive problems, respiratory infections, and skin conditions. Grapes were grown in many regions of Europe, including Italy, France, and Spain.

11 Herbs and Spices Found in Medieval Gardens

Medieval gardens were filled with a variety of herbs and spices that were used for culinary, medicinal, and aromatic purposes. Some of the most popular herbs and spices in medieval gardens included sweet bay, sweet myrtle, rosemary, sage, thyme, winter savory, lavender, marjoram, fennel, and parsley. These plants were often grown in companion with other plants and required specific conditions for optimal growth. They were a testament to the importance of gardens in medieval life and their legacy can still be seen in modern gardens today.

1. Sweet Bay
- **Variety:** *Laurus nobilis*
- **Country most often seen:** Italy, England
- **Companion plants:** Rosemary, sage, thyme
- **Conditions required for optimal growth:** Full sun to partial shade, well-drained soil
- **Uses:** Culinary, medicinal
- **Lore:** Sweet bay was believed to have the power to ward off evil spirits and was often used in medieval times to make wreaths for athletes and scholars.

2. Sweet Myrtle
- **Variety**: *Myrtus communis*
- **Country most often seen:** Italy, England
- **Companion plants:** Rosemary, sage, thyme
- **Conditions required for optimal growth**: Full sun to partial shade, well-drained soil
- **Uses:** Culinary, medicinal
- **Lore:** Sweet myrtle was considered a symbol of love and was often used in wedding ceremonies in medieval times.

3. Rosemary
- **Variety**: *Rosmarinus officinalis*
- **Country most often seen**: Italy, England
- **Companion plants**: Sage, thyme, lavender
- **Conditions required for optimal growth:** Full sun, well-drained soil
- **Uses:** Culinary, medicinal, aromatic
- **Lore**: Rosemary was believed to have memory-enhancing properties and was often used by students during exams in medieval times.

4. Sage
- **Variety:** *Salvia officinalis*
- **Country most often seen:** Italy, England
- **Companion plants:** Rosemary, thyme, lavender
- **Conditions required for optimal growth:** Full sun, well-drained soil
- **Uses:** Culinary, medicinal, aromatic
- **Lore:** Sage was believed to have healing properties and was often used to treat a variety of ailments, including sore throats and digestive issues.
- **Fun Fact:** In medieval Europe, sage was believed to have protective and purifying properties. It was often used in rituals to cleanse spaces and objects of negative energy or spirits. Sprigs of sage were sometimes burned as a form of incense to ward off evil and bring positive energy. Sage's use as a protective herb was especially prevalent during the medieval period.

5. Thyme
- **Variety:** *Thymus vulgaris*
- **Country most often seen:** Italy, England
- **Companion plants:** Rosemary, sage, lavender
- **Conditions required for optimal growth:** Full sun, well-drained soil
- **Uses:** Culinary, medicinal, aromatic
- **Lore:** Thyme was believed to have antiseptic properties and was often used to treat wounds and infections in medieval times.
- **Fun Fact:** Knights and chivalry were prominent in medieval Europe, and thyme was often associated with these ideals. It was customary for medieval knights to wear sprigs of thyme in their armor, or to include thyme in their pouches and handkerchiefs, as a symbol of bravery and strength. Thyme's aromatic and medicinal properties also made it a practical choice for this purpose.

6. Winter Savory
- **Variety:** *Satureja montana*
- **Country most often seen:** England
- **Companion plants:** Thyme, rosemary, sage
- **Conditions required for optimal growth:** Full sun, well-drained soil
- **Uses:** Culinary, medicinal
- **Lore:** Winter savory was believed to have aphrodisiac properties and was often used in love potions in medieval times. Winter savory, like several other herbs and spices, contains natural compounds with antimicrobial properties. These compounds can inhibit the growth of bacteria and fungi that cause food spoilage. By adding winter savory to dishes or using it to season and marinate foods, medieval cooks could help extend the shelf life of their meals.

7. Lavender
- **Variety:** *Lavandula angustifolia*
- **Country most often seen:** England
- **Companion plants:** Rosemary, sage, thyme
- **Conditions required for optimal growth:** Full sun, well-drained soil
- **Uses:** Culinary, medicinal, aromatic
- **Lore:** Lavender was believed to have calming properties and was often used to treat anxiety and insomnia in medieval times.

8. Marjoram
- **Variety:** *Origanum majorana*
- **Country most often seen:** Italy, England
- **Companion plants:** Thyme, rosemary, sage
- **Conditions required for optimal growth:** Full sun, well-drained soil
- **Uses:** Culinary, medicinal
- **Lore:** Marjoram was believed to have digestive properties and was often used to treat stomach issues in medieval times.

10. Parsley
- **Variety:** *Petroselinum crispum*
- **Country most often seen:** Italy, England
- **Companion plants:** Fennel, dill, coriander
- **Conditions required for optimal growth:** Full sun, well-drained soil
- **Uses:** Culinary, medicinal
- **Lore:** Parsley was believed to have cleansing properties and was often used to freshen breath and aid digestion in medieval times.

11. Fennel
- **Variety:** *Foeniculum vulgare*
- **Country most often found:** Fennel is native to the Mediterranean region, but it was also commonly found in medieval gardens in other parts of Europe, including Italy and England
- **Uses for the plant:** Fennel is a sweet aromatic herb that is used for culinary and medicinal purposes. It has a licorice-like flavor and is often used in salads, soups, and stews. It is also used to flavor liqueurs and other beverages. Medicinally, fennel has been used to treat digestive issues, menstrual cramps, and respiratory infections.
- **Companion plants:** Fennel is often grown in companion with other plants, such as dill, parsley, and coriander.
- **Conditions for optimal growth:** Fennel grows best in full sun and well-drained soil. It can tolerate some shade, but too much shade can cause it to become leggy and weak. Fennel is a hardy plant that can survive in a range of soil types, but it prefers soil that is rich in organic matter.
- **Lore:** Fennel was considered one of the nine sacred curative herbs of medieval times and was believed to protect against evil spirits when hung over doorways.

Onions

A little-known fact about onions is that they were used as a form of currency in ancient Egypt. Onions were highly regarded by the Egyptians for their nutritional value and versatility in cooking. They were even placed in the tombs of pharaohs, such as King Tutankhamun, to sustain them in the afterlife. As a measure of their value, onions were sometimes used to pay the laborers who built the pyramids. This historical use of onions as currency highlights their significance in the daily life and culture of ancient Egypt.

Onions: A Special Mention

Onions were an important crop in the Middle Ages, and they played a significant role in the daily lives of people during that time. Here are some reasons why onions were so important:

1. Currency:
Onions were so valuable in the Middle Ages that people often paid their rent with them and gave them as gifts. They were considered a form of currency, and their value was recognized by many. Onions were also used as payment for services rendered, such as for the construction of buildings or for the work of laborers.

2. Food:
Onions were a staple food in the Middle Ages, and they were used in a variety of dishes. They were often added to stews, soups, and other dishes to add flavor and nutrition. Onions were also used to make sauces and condiments, such as onion jam and onion relish.

3. Medicine:
Onions were believed to have medicinal properties in the Middle Ages, and they were used to treat a variety of ailments. They were used to alleviate headaches, snakebites, and hair loss. Onions were also believed to have antibacterial properties, and they were used to treat infections.

4. Warding Off Illness:
Onions were believed to have protective qualities against various illnesses. Placing onions in a room or hanging them around one's neck was thought to purify the air by absorbing bacteria and pathogens. This belief was based on the observation that onions would sometimes rot or turn black when exposed to harmful air, reinforcing the notion that they absorbed toxins. While these beliefs were not scientifically proven, they reflected the importance of onions in medieval culture as a symbol of health and wellbeing.

5. Storage:
Onions were easy to grow and could be dried for storage without refrigeration or smoking or salting. This made them an ideal crop for people in the Middle Ages, who needed to store food for long periods of time.

6. Symbolism:
Onions were also used as a symbol in the Middle Ages. They were associated with eternity because of their circle-within-a-circle structure, and they were often used in religious ceremonies.

Onions continue to be an important crop, and they are used in a variety of dishes around the world.

Fruits and Vegetables in Medieval Gardens

Medieval gardens were not only filled with flowers but also with a variety of fruits and vegetables. Here are some examples of fruits and vegetables typically found in medieval gardens:

1. Carrots
- Varieties: *Daucus carota*
- Countries most often found: Europe, Asia
- Ideal growing conditions: Full sun to partial shade, well-drained soil
- Companion plants: Onions, leeks, garlic
- Uses: Culinary, medicinal
- Folklore: Carrots were considered a vegetable of the poor until the Renaissance. They were believed to have healing properties and were used to treat a variety of ailments.

2. Peas
- Varieties: *Pisum sativum*
- Countries most often found: Europe, Asia
- Ideal growing conditions: Full sun to partial shade, well-drained soil
- Companion plants: Beans, carrots, lettuce
- Uses: Culinary
- Folklore: Peas were a basic food in the Middle Ages, along with grains and beans. They were often dried, which allowed them to be preserved and to serve as a precious resource during times of famine.

3. Cauliflower
- Varieties: *Brassica oleracea var. botrytis*
- Countries most often found: Europe, Asia
- Ideal growing conditions: Full sun to partial shade, well-drained soil
- Companion plants: Onions, garlic, leeks
- Uses: Culinary
- Folklore: Cauliflower was a substantial peasant food in the Middle Ages and became the emblem of a popular, healthy diet.

4. Artichokes
- Varieties: *Cynara cardunculus var. scolymus*
- Countries most often found: Mediterranean region
- Ideal growing conditions: Full sun, well-drained soil
- Companion plants: Beans, peas, lettuce
- Uses: Culinary, medicinal
- Folklore: Artichokes were believed to have healing properties and were used to treat a variety of ailments.

5. Cabbage
- Varieties: *Brassica oleracea var. capitata*
- Countries most often found: Europe, Asia
- Ideal growing conditions: Full sun to partial shade, well-drained soil

- Companion plants: Onions, garlic, leeks
- Uses: Culinary, medicinal
- Folklore: Cabbage was a staple food in the Middle Ages and was believed to have healing properties.

6. Apples
- Varieties: *Malus domestica*
- Countries most often found: Europe, Asia
- Ideal growing conditions: Full sun, well-drained soil
- Companion plants: Pears, plums, cherries
- Uses: Culinary, medicinal
- Folklore: Apples were associated with the Greek goddess Aphrodite and were often used in religious ceremonies. They were also believed to have healing properties and were used to treat a variety of ailments.

7. Pears
- Varieties: *Pyrus communis*
- Countries most often found: Europe, Asia
- Ideal growing conditions: Full sun, well-drained soil
- Companion plants: Apples, plums, cherries
- Uses: Culinary, medicinal
- Folklore: Pears were associated with the Greek goddess Hera and were often used in religious ceremonies. They were also believed to have healing properties and were used to treat a variety of ailments.

8. Plums
- Varieties: *Prunus domestica*
- Countries most often found: Europe, Asia
- Ideal growing conditions: Full sun, well-drained soil
- Companion plants: Apples, pears, cherries
- Uses: Culinary, medicinal
- Folklore: Plums were associated with the Greek god Dionysus and were often used in religious ceremonies. They were also believed to have healing properties and were used to treat a variety of ailments.

9. Cherries
- Varieties: *Prunus avium*
- Countries most often found: Europe, Asia
- Ideal growing conditions: Full sun, well-drained soil
- Companion plants: Apples, pears, plums
- Uses: Culinary, medicinal
- Folklore: Cherries were associated with the Greek goddess Demeter and were often used in religious ceremonies. They were also believed to have healing properties and were used to treat a variety of ailments.

10. Onions
- Varieties: *Allium cepa*
- Countries most often found: Europe, Asia

- Ideal growing conditions: Full sun, well-drained soil
- Companion plants: Carrots, peas, beans
- Uses: Culinary, medicinal
- Folklore: Onions were believed to have healing properties and were used to treat a variety of ailments. They were also associated with the Greek god Apollo and were often used in religious ceremonies.

Not Enough Options?

Medieval gardens were filled with a variety of fruits and vegetables. Here are 20 more examples of fruits and vegetables typically found in medieval gardens:

1. Beans
- **Varieties:** *Phaseolus vulgaris*
- **Countries most often found:** Europe, Asia
- **Ideal growing conditions:** Full sun, well-drained soil
- **Companion plants:** Peas, carrots, lettuce
- **Uses:** Culinary
- **Folklore:** Beans were a basic food in the Middle Ages, along with grains and peas. They were often dried, which allowed them to be preserved and to serve as a precious resource during times of famine.
- **Anecdote:** in many villages, a large cauldron of bean pottage would be prepared and shared among the villagers. Each family contributed some ingredients, often whatever they had on hand, to create a collective meal. This practice fostered a sense of community and ensured that even those with limited resources could enjoy a hearty and nutritious meal.
  - The sharing of bean pottage was a way for medieval communities to come together, support one another, and make the most of their available food resources. It reflects the importance of beans as a staple food during that time and the communal spirit that often prevailed in medieval European villages.

2. Lettuce
- **Varieties:** *Lactuca sativa*
- **Countries most often found:** Europe, Asia
- **Ideal growing conditions**: Partial shade to full sun, well-drained soil
- **Companion plants:** Peas, beans, carrots
- **Uses:** Culinary, medicinal
- **Folklore:** Lettuce was believed to have healing properties and was used to treat a variety of ailments.

3. Radishes
- **Varieties:** *Raphanus sativus*
- **Countries most often found:** Europe, Asia
- **Ideal growing conditions:** Full sun, well-drained soil
- **Companion plants:** Carrots, peas, beans

Carrots, Lettuce and Radish

In medieval Europe, carrots were primarily used for medicinal purposes and were often grown for their seeds, which were believed to have healing properties. It wasn't until the 16th century in the Netherlands that orange carrots were bred to celebrate the Dutch Royal Family's color, leading to the familiar orange variety we know today.

Lettuce is one of the oldest cultivated plants in the world, with origins traced back to ancient Egypt over 4,000 years ago. It was highly prized by the Egyptians and used in religious ceremonies, as well as for culinary purposes.

Radishes were a common vegetable in medieval Europe and were valued for their quick growth, making them an essential food source during times of scarcity. They were also used as a treatment for various ailments in traditional medicine. They have been cultivated for over 2,000 years and were introduced to Europe by the Romans.

- Uses: Culinary, medicinal
- Folklore: Radishes were believed to have healing properties and were used to treat a variety of ailments.

4. Turnips
- **Varieties:** *Brassica rapa*
- **Countries most often found:** Europe, Asia
- **Ideal growing conditions:** Full sun to partial shade, well-drained soil
- **Companion plants:** Carrots, peas, beans
- **Uses:** Culinary, medicinal
- **Folklore:** Turnips were a staple food in the Middle Ages and were believed to have healing properties.

5. Garlic
- **Varieties:** *Allium sativum*
- **Countries most often found:** Europe, Asia
- **Ideal growing conditions:** Full sun, well-drained soil
- **Companion plants:** Onions, leeks, carrots
- **Uses:** Culinary, medicinal
- **Folklore:** Garlic was believed to have healing properties and was used to treat a variety of ailments.
- **History:** In ancient Greece, Olympic athletes consumed garlic to enhance their performance. Garlic was believed to boost strength and stamina, making it a natural performance enhancer for the games.
- **Garlic and Superstitions:** Garlic has had its share of superstitions. In some cultures, garlic was placed under children's pillows to protect them from evil spirits. It was also believed to protect against the evil eye.
- **Garlic in World War I:** During World War I, garlic was used to treat wounds because of its antiseptic properties. It was applied to wounds to prevent infection and promote healing.

7. Parsnips
- **Varieties:** *Pastinaca sativa*
- **Countries most often found:** Europe, Asia
- **Ideal growing conditions**: Full sun to partial shade, well-drained soil
- **Companion plants:** Carrots, peas, beans
- **Uses:** Culinary, medicinal
- **Folklore:** Parsnips were a staple food in the Middle Ages and were believed to have healing properties. In medieval times, parsnips were sometimes used for love divination. Young women believed that they could predict their romantic future by the shape of parsnips they pulled from the ground. A straight, unbroken parsnip was seen as a sign of a good, faithful partner, while a forked or twisted parsnip might suggest a problematic or unfaithful relationship.

6. Leeks
- **Varieties:** *Allium ampeloprasum*
- **Countries most often found:** Europe, Asia
- **Ideal growing conditions:** Full sun to partial shade, well-drained soil
- **Companion plants:** Onions, garlic, carrots
- **Uses:** Culinary, medicinal
- **Folklore:** Leeks were a staple food in the Middle Ages and were believed to have healing properties.

William Shakespeare mentioned leeks in his play "Henry V." In Act 5, Scene 1, commonly referred to as the "St. Crispin's Day Speech," King Henry V delivers a powerful and inspirational speech to his troops before the Battle of Agincourt.

He uses leeks as a symbol of unity and camaraderie among the English soldiers:

"This day is called the feast of Crispian:
He that outlives this day, and comes safe home,
Will stand a tip-toe when the day is named,
And rouse him at the name of Crispian.
He that shall live this day, and see old age,
Will yearly on the vigil feast his neighbours,
And say 'To-morrow is Saint Crispian:'
Then will he strip his sleeve and show his scars.
And say 'These wounds I had on Crispin's day.'
Old men forget: yet all shall be forgot,
But he'll remember with advantages
What feats he did that day: then shall our names.
Familiar in his mouth as household words
Harry the king, Bedford and Exeter,
Warwick and Talbot, Salisbury and Gloucester,
Be in their flowing cups freshly remember'd.
This story shall the good man teach his son;
And Crispin Crispian shall ne'er go by,
From this day to the ending of the world,
But we in it shall be remember'd:
We few, we happy few, we band of brothers;
For he to-day that sheds his blood with me
Shall be my brother; be he ne'er so vile,
This day shall gentle his condition."

In this passage, King Henry V uses the feast of St. Crispin as a symbol of unity and valor, suggesting that those who fight with him on this day will be forever bound together in brotherhood. The reference to leeks is part of the imagery of the feast, emphasizing the shared experience and camaraderie of the soldiers.

8. Figs
- **Varieties:** *Ficus carica*
- **Countries most often found:** Mediterranean region
- **Ideal growing conditions:** Full sun, well-drained soil
- **Companion plants:** Grapes, pomegranates, olives
- **Uses:** Culinary, medicinal
- **Folklore:** Figs were associated with the Greek god Dionysus and were often used in religious ceremonies. They were also believed to have healing properties and were used to treat a variety of ailments.

9. Grapes
- **Varieties:** *Vitis vinifera*
- **Countries most often found:** Europe, Asia
- **Ideal growing conditions:** Full sun, well-drained soil
- **Companion plants:** Figs, pomegranates, olives
- **Uses:** Culinary, medicinal
- **Folklore:** Grapes were associated with the Greek god Dionysus and were often used in religious ceremonies. They were also believed to have healing properties and were used to treat a variety of ailments.

10. Pomegranates
- **Varieties:** *Punica granatum*
- **Countries most often found:** Mediterranean region
- **Ideal growing conditions:** Full sun, well-drained soil
- **Companion plants:** Figs, grapes, olives
- **Uses:** Culinary, medicinal
- **Folklore:** Pomegranates were associated with the Greek goddess Persephone and were often used in religious ceremonies. They were also believed to have healing properties and were used to treat a variety of ailments.

11. Almonds
- **Varieties:** *Prunus dulcis*
- **Countries most often found:** Mediterranean region
- **Ideal growing conditions:** Full sun, well-drained soil
- **Companion plants:** Olives, figs, pomegranates
- **Uses:** Culinary, medicinal
- **Folklore:** Almonds were associated with the Greek myth of Phyllis and were often used in religious ceremonies. They were also believed to have healing properties and were used to treat a variety of ailments.

12. Walnuts
- **Varieties:** *Juglans regia*
- **Countries most often found:** Europe, Asia
- **Ideal growing conditions:** Full sun, well-drained soil
- **Companion plants:** Apples, pears, cherries
- **Uses:** Culinary, medicinal
- **Folklore:** Walnuts were associated with the Greek god Zeus and were

often used in religious ceremonies. They were also believed to have healing properties and were used to treat a variety of ailments.
- **Other:** The English walnut, scientifically known as Juglans regia, is not native to England but was introduced there from Persia in the 16th century. This variety of walnut became popular in England and Europe, and it's the one commonly found in culinary applications today.
- **Festivals:** Walnut festivals can be found in different European countries, including France, Italy, and Spain, where walnut cultivation has a long history. Each region may have its unique traditions and ways of celebrating the walnut harvest.
- Walnut festivals are typically held during the walnut harvest season, which varies depending on the region but often falls in the late summer or early autumn. The festivals are an opportunity for local communities to come together and celebrate the bounty of their walnut orchards.
- Walnut festivals are known for their culinary offerings. Visitors can enjoy a variety of walnut-based dishes and treats, from sweet pastries like walnut tarts and cakes to savory dishes such as walnut-stuffed ravioli or roasted walnuts with herbs.

13. Quinces
- **Varieties:** *Cydonia oblonga*
- **Countries most often found:** Mediterranean region
- **Ideal growing conditions:** Full sun, well-drained soil
- **Companion plants:** Apples, pears, cherries
- **Uses:** Culinary, medicinal
- **Folklore:** Quinces were associated with the Greek goddess Aphrodite and were Other history: often used in religious ceremonies. They were also believed to have healing properties and were used to treat a variety of ailments.
- **History:** In medieval Europe, quinces were highly regarded for their exotic flavor and aromatic qualities. They were often used to make a delicacy known as "cotignac," a sweet quince paste that was a favorite among European nobility.

Legend has it that Queen Eleanor of Aquitaine, known for her refined tastes, was particularly fond of quince cotignac. She had a prized recipe that she guarded closely. However, during a visit to her court, a mischievous courtier decided to sneak a peek at the queen's recipe book.

To his surprise, he found the quince cotignac recipe, but instead of writing down the entire instructions, he omitted a crucial step. The courtier left out the part about adding sugar, thinking he could create a delicious treat for himself without the queen's knowledge.

The next time Queen Eleanor requested quince cotignac, she was shocked to discover that her beloved treat had turned into a bitter and inedible concoction. The courtier's plan had backfired, and he had inadvertently played a prank on the queen.

14. Cucumbers
- **Varieties:** *Cucumis sativus*
- **Countries most often found:** Europe, Asia
- **Ideal growing conditions:** Full sun, well-drained soil
- **Companion plants:** Beans, peas, lettuce
- **Uses:** Culinary, medicinal
- **Folklore:** Cucumbers were believed to have healing properties and were used to treat a variety of ailments. One humorous historical aspect related to cucumbers is the once-held belief in some European regions that cucumbers could cause madness or provoke strange dreams if consumed too late in the day. This superstition led to amusing cautionary tales about the perils of eating cucumbers after sunset.

15. Melons
- **Varieties:** *Cucumis melo*
- **Countries most often found:** Europe, Asia
- **Ideal growing conditions:** Full sun, well-drained soil
- **Companion plants:** Beans, peas, lettuce
- **Uses:** Culinary, medicinal. Melons were sometimes preserved in honey or sugar syrups to extend their shelf life and enhance their flavor. These preserves could be used in various culinary preparations, including tarts, pies, and sweet pastries.
- **Folklore:** Melons were associated with the Greek god Dionysus and were often used in religious ceremonies. They were also believed to have healing properties and were used to treat a variety of ailments.

16. Strawberries
- **Varieties:** *Fragaria x ananassa*
- **Countries most often found:** Europe, Asia
- **Ideal growing conditions:** Full sun to partial shade, well-drained soil
- **Companion plants:** Lettuce, beans, peas
- **Uses:** Culinary, medicinal
- **Folklore:** Strawberries were associated with the Greek goddess Aphrodite and were often used in religious ceremonies.
- **Later day story:** In the 18th century, a French military engineer named Amédée-François Frézier embarked on a mission to steal a treasure coveted by his country: the Chilean strawberry. At the time, France had no access to these exquisite berries. Disguised as a Spanish friar, Frézier smuggled Chilean strawberry plants back to France. However, these Chilean strawberries weren't quite as expected; they were small and tart. Frézier diligently crossbred them with other varieties, and after years of effort, the sweet and succulent "Fraises de Chile" emerged, forever changing the world of strawberries. His daring strawberry heist left a legacy that still tantalizes taste buds today.

Strawberries

In the late 19th century, Amos Pickney of Haverhill, Massachusetts, started experimenting with strawberry breeding. He was determined to create a strawberry variety that was not only large but also flavorful and resilient. After years of careful crossbreeding, he succeeded in creating what would become known as the "California Giant" strawberry.

This new strawberry variety featured exceptionally large fruit, vibrant red color, and a sweet, juicy taste. It also proved to be more resistant to diseases and pests than many other strawberry varieties of the time. Recognizing its potential, Pickney decided to introduce his creation to the world.

In 1882, he sent a package of California Giant strawberry plants to a friend in California. The friend planted them, and the strawberries thrived in the California climate. Soon, the California Giant strawberry gained widespread attention for its impressive size and flavor.

The California Giant strawberry became a sensation and played a crucial role in the growth of the strawberry industry in California. Today, it is considered one of the ancestors of the modern commercial strawberry varieties.

IV

Long Pepper

The introduction of long pepper to Europe can be traced back to ancient trade routes that connected Asia to the Mediterranean world. Historical records suggest that long pepper was being traded with the Roman Empire as early as the 1st century CE. It was one of the coveted spices, alongside black pepper, that drove the spice trade along the Silk Road and maritime routes.

Long pepper found its way to Europe primarily through trade with the Byzantine Empire and the Arab world. By the medieval period, it had firmly established itself as a sought-after spice in European culinary and medicinal practices.

While long pepper was widely used in Europe during the Middle Ages and the Renaissance, its popularity gradually waned in favor of black pepper and other spices. By the early modern period, long pepper had become less common in European kitchens, but it left a lasting influence on historical recipes and culinary traditions. Today, long pepper has seen a resurgence in popularity as part of the broader interest in rediscovering and reinterpreting historical ingredients and flavors in contemporary cuisine.

Long Pepper *Piper longum*

Long pepper, scientifically known as *Piper longum*, has a storied history dating back over two thousand years. Originating in Southeast Asia, it was used in ancient India for both culinary and medicinal purposes, prominently featured in Ayurvedic texts. This versatile spice gained popularity in ancient Rome and Greece, with mentions in the Roman cookbook "Apicius." During medieval Europe, it was treasured but gave way to the dominance of black pepper due to its scarcity. However, in recent years, long pepper has experienced a resurgence among chefs for its unique spicy-sweet-floral flavor profile, adding a touch of history and distinction to modern culinary creations.

Long Pepper has a rich history dating back thousands of years.

Long Pepper, scientifically known as *Piper longum*, is a spice with a long history of use in culinary and medicinal traditions. Uncommon today, if not completely unknown, it was a Medieval culinary staple.

Latin Name: *Piper longum*

History:

1. Ancient Spice:
Long pepper is one of the oldest known spices, with a history dating back over two thousand years. It was cultivated and traded extensively in ancient India and other parts of Southeast Asia. Long pepper was mentioned in ancient Indian texts, including Ayurvedic texts, where it was used for its medicinal properties.

2. Roman and Greek Use:
Long pepper was highly prized in ancient Rome and Greece. It was used both as a spice and for its medicinal properties. The famous Roman cookbook "Apicius" contains recipes that include long pepper, demonstrating its culinary significance in Roman cuisine.

3. Middle Ages and Medieval Europe:
Long pepper was a valuable and sought-after spice in medieval Europe, along with other exotic spices from the East. It was used to flavor food and beverages, and it had a significant presence in the spice trade. Due to its scarcity and high cost, it was considered a luxury item.

4. Decline in Popularity:
Over time, the popularity of long pepper waned in Europe as black pepper, which was easier to cultivate and transport, became the dominant peppercorn. Long pepper became less common in European cuisine but remained important in certain Asian culinary traditions.

5. Revival:
In recent years, long pepper has experienced a revival in culinary circles. It is prized by chefs for its unique flavor profile, which includes spiciness with hints of sweet and floral notes. It is often used in gourmet dishes, artisanal spice blends, and craft cocktails.

Long pepper's Latin name, *Piper longum*, reflects its botanical relationship to black pepper (*Piper nigrum*). While black pepper remains the more widely used peppercorn, long pepper continues to be appreciated for its historical significance and distinctive flavor, making it a unique addition to the world of spices and seasonings.

Long pepper is a spice that was commonly used in medieval cuisine. The use of spices was an important aspect of medieval cuisine, as they were used to add flavor to food and to mask the taste of spoiled ingredients, and it was commonly used in medieval cuisine to add heat and flavor to dishes

Spices such as pepper and cinnamon were commonly used in medieval cuisine, and they were often imported from distant lands, making them expensive and a status symbol for the wealthy. The nobility's food was more prone to foreign influence than the cuisine of the poor, and it was dependent on exotic spices and expensive imports.

Long Pepper Folklore

Long pepper has a rich history and has been used for medicinal and dietary purposes for centuries.

- In ancient Indian textbooks of Ayurveda, long pepper is described in detail for its medicinal and dietary uses. It was believed to have warming and digestive qualities that could help with various ailments.

- Long pepper was often mistaken for black pepper in ancient times, and it was used in Indian, Thai, Cambodian, and Indonesian cuisine[2]. It was also used in ancient Greek and Roman cuisine, where it was an important and well-known spice.

- Long pepper is beautiful to look at, resembling slender, elegant pine-cones that are about an inch long. When snapped in two, the inside is a cluster of tiny seeds.

- Long pepper is also known as pippali, Bengal pepper, and Indonesian pepper. It is a very slender, perennial, and aromatic climber that grows well in the shade of trees. This spice is also cultivated in Assam, West Bengal, Nepal, and Uttar Pradesh.

- Long pepper is believed to have aphrodisiac properties, and it was used in ancient times to enhance sexual desire and performance. It was also believed to have anti-inflammatory and anti-bacterial properties.

Growing Conditions

Long pepper grows well in tropical and subtropical regions, and it requires a long growing season of around 75 days. The plant prefers well-drained soil that is rich in organic matter. It can grow in full sun or partial shade, but it prefers the latter. Long pepper is a climbing plant that requires support, such as a trellis or a fence, to grow properly. You will not be able to grow this without a very hot and humid greenhouse.

Medicinal Properties of Long Pepper

Long pepper, also known as *Piper longum*, has been used for its medicinal properties for thousands of years. In Ayurvedic medicine, long pepper is considered one of the most important herbs, and its roots and fruits are used for their medicinal properties. Examples:

- **Digestive health:** Long pepper has been used to treat digestive issues, such as indigestion, bloating, and constipation. It is believed to stimulate the digestive fire and improve digestion.

- **Respiratory health:** Long pepper has been used to treat respiratory problems, such as coughs, asthma, and bronchitis. It is believed to help clear the respiratory passages and reduce inflammation.

- **Fever:** Long pepper has been used to treat fever, as it is believed to have antipyretic properties.

- **Sexual health:** Long pepper has been used as an aphrodisiac and sexual enhancer. According to the Kama Sutra, a mixture of long pepper, black pepper, datura, and honey, will allow a man to 'bewitch and subjugate his partners'.

Modern research has also shown that long pepper has a range of health benefits. Here are some examples:

- **Anti-inflammatory properties:** Long pepper contains piperlongumine, a compound that has been shown to have anti-inflammatory properties.

- **Antioxidant properties:** Long pepper contains flavonoids and other compounds that have antioxidant properties.

- **Anti-cancer properties:** Long pepper has been shown to have anti-cancer properties, particularly against breast cancer cells.

- **Anti-diabetic properties:** Long pepper has been shown to have anti-diabetic properties, as it can help regulate blood sugar levels.

Long pepper has also been compared to other medicinal plants, such as black pepper and ginger.

- **Black Pepper:** Long pepper is similar to black pepper in taste and aroma, but it is hotter and more pungent. Both peppers have similar medicinal properties, such as digestive and respiratory health benefits.

- **Ginger:** Long pepper is similar to ginger in taste and aroma, but it is hotter and more pungent. Both plants have similar medicinal properties, such as anti-inflammatory and digestive health benefits.

Culinary Uses for Long Pepper

Long pepper, also known as *Piper longum*, has been used in culinary applications for thousands of years. It was a popular spice in ancient and medieval cuisine, and it is still used in global cuisine today. Here are some historical uses of long pepper in ancient and medieval cuisine:

Ancient India: Long pepper was used in ancient Indian cuisine, particularly in lentil stews and pickles.

Ancient Greece and Rome: Long pepper was a popular spice in ancient Greece and Rome, where it was used in cooking and to make mulled medicinal wine.

Medieval Europe: Long pepper was used in medieval European cuisine, particularly in stews, sauces, and meat dishes.

Modern uses of long pepper in global cuisine include Indian, Thai, Cambodian, and Indonesian cooking. It is used in stews, spice mixes, grilled meats, barbecue sauces, and lightly cooked vegetables.

Here are some comparisons of Long Pepper with other spices:

Black Pepper:
Long pepper is hotter and more pungent than black pepper, and it has a more complex flavor profile that includes nuances of ginger, cinnamon, nutmeg, and cardamom.

Long pepper has a more complex and nuanced flavor profile than black pepper.

Here are some of the differences in flavor between long pepper and black pepper:

- Long pepper has a sweet taste, while black pepper has a more pungent taste.

- Long pepper has earthy undertones and a sly sweetness, while black pepper has a more aggressive and bitter taste.

- Long pepper has a more complex flavor profile, reminiscent of spice blends like garam masala, while black pepper has a simpler taste.

- Long pepper has a heat that is similar to black pepper, but it is less harsh and more nuanced. It is tempered by sweet notes of nutmeg, cinnamon, and cardamom.

- Long pepper has a tobacco-like coolness that lingers on the tongue, while black pepper stings.

Long Pepper has also been compared to Grains of Paradise and Ginger.

Grains of Paradise:
Grains of Paradise and Long Pepper, while both belonging to the realm of exotic spices, offer distinct tastes and culinary applications.

Grains of Paradise are known for their warm and slightly citrusy flavor, evoking a mild spiciness with hints of cardamom and black pepper. This flavor profile makes them a versatile ingredient, adding complexity to dishes, whether savory or sweet.

In contrast, Long Pepper presents a more robust and fiery taste, with an earthy heat that builds slowly. This spicier quality makes it a favored component in traditional Asian, Indian, and medieval European cuisines, where it's used to lend a distinctive, spicier note to spice blends like garam masala.

Both spices have unique and desirable characteristics, making them valuable additions to the spice rack for those looking to explore and experiment with distinct flavor profiles in their culinary creations.

Ginger:
Long pepper is similar to ginger in taste and aroma, but it is hotter and more pungent.

Modern Uses

Long pepper is a spice that is still used in modern cuisine, although it is not as common as black pepper. Here are some ways that long pepper is used in modern cuisine:

In Indian cuisine, long pepper is used in lentil stews and pickles, and its sweet heat takes well to Southeast Asian-style roasted meats. It is also used in chicken dishes, such as Long Pepper Chicken.

Long pepper can be used as a substitute for regular black pepper in a variety of dishes, such as stews, spice mixes, grilled meats, and lightly cooked vegetables.

Long pepper has a more complex flavor profile than black pepper, with nuances of ginger, cinnamon, nutmeg, and cardamom. It can be used to add a unique spice to dishes and to enhance the flavor of barbecue sauce.

Long pepper is also used in pickles, preserves, and other condiments on a global scale.

Long pepper is cultivated in Assam, West Bengal, Nepal, and Uttar Pradesh, and it is available on-line and at specialty spice shops.

How to Use Long Pepper in Today's Kitchen

Long Pepper, known for its distinct and spicier flavor, can be used to add depth and complexity to a variety of dishes. Here are some of the ways you can bring this almost unknown pleasure to your dining table or event.

Savory Dishes

1. Spice Blends: Long Pepper can be a key ingredient in spice blends such as garam masala and Thai curry pastes.

2. Marinades: Create a Long Pepper marinade for meats like chicken, lamb, or pork.

3. Sauces: Add ground Long Pepper to your barbecue or stir-fry sauces for a spicier kick.

4. Stews: Long Pepper can be included in hearty stews and soups for added warmth and flavor.

5. Rice Dishes: Season rice, pilaf, or biryani with Long Pepper for a unique taste.

6. Grilled Vegetables: Use it in seasoning mixes for grilled vegetables like zucchini, eggplant, or bell peppers.

7. Seafood: Incorporate Long Pepper into seafood dishes, like pan-seared scallops or shrimp scampi.

Baking and Desserts

8. Cookies: Add a pinch of ground Long Pepper to ginger or molasses cookies.

9. Fruit Desserts: Sprinkle Long Pepper on grilled pineapple or baked apples.

10. Cakes: Experiment with Long Pepper in spice cakes and carrot cakes.

11. Chocolates: Infuse Long Pepper into dark chocolate ganache or truffles for a hint of spiciness.

Beverages

12. Cocktails: Make a "Long Pepper and Lime" cocktail by muddling Long Pepper with lime, adding gin, and a splash of simple syrup.

13. Infused Syrups: Create Long Pepper-infused syrups for use in various cocktails and mocktails.

14. Hot Beverages: Infuse Long Pepper in hot chocolate or chai tea for a warming twist.

5. Smoothies: Add a pinch of ground Long Pepper to fruit smoothies for an unexpected kick.

The Unexpected

16. Gingerbread Cake: The Balinese long pepper is used in gingerbread cake to add a sweet and fiery flavor.

17. Pfeffernüsse: Pfeffernüsse are traditional German cookies that use long pepper as a key ingredient. They are spiced with cinnamon, cloves, and long pepper, and they have a sweet and spicy flavor.

18. Fruit Compote: Long pepper can be used to add a sweet and spicy flavor to fruit compote. It pairs well with fruits like apples, pears, and plums.

19. Ice Cream: Long pepper can be used to add a unique spice to ice cream. It pairs well with flavors like vanilla, chocolate, and caramel.

20. Chocolate Truffles: Long pepper can be used to add a sweet and spicy flavor to chocolate truffles. It pairs well with dark chocolate and adds a unique twist to the classic dessert.

The Cocktail

Long Pepper and Lime Cocktail

Ingredients

- 2-3 Long Pepper spikes (or 1/4 teaspoon ground Long Pepper)
- 2 oz gin
- 1 oz fresh lime juice
- 1/2 oz simple syrup
- Ice
- Lime wheel or twist, for garnish

Instructions

1. Muddle the Long Pepper spikes in a cocktail shaker.
2. Add the gin, fresh lime juice, and simple syrup to the shaker.
3. Fill the shaker with ice and shake vigorously until well chilled.
4. Strain the mixture into a chilled cocktail glass.
5. Garnish with a lime wheel or twist.
6. Enjoy your Long Pepper and Lime cocktail!

This cocktail balances the spicy warmth of Long Pepper with the bright acidity of lime and the sweetness of simple syrup for a delightful and aromatic drink.

Long Pepper and Sea Salt Molten Chocolate Cake

Ingredients

- 4 oz/115 g unsalted butter, cubed plus a little extra to grease the ramekins
- 2 tsp all-purpose flour plus a little extra to dust the ramekins
- 4 oz/115 g semisweet chocolate, chopped
- 2 large eggs
- 1/4 cup granulated sugar
- 1/8 tsp sea salt
- 1/2 tsp ground long pepper

Instructions

1. Preheat the oven to 425°F. Grease four 4-ounce ramekins with butter and dust them with flour.

2. In a small saucepan, melt the butter and chocolate over low heat, stirring until smooth. Remove from heat and let cool for 5 minutes.

3. In a medium bowl, whisk together the eggs, sugar, sea salt, and ground long pepper until well combined.

4. Add the chocolate mixture to the egg mixture and whisk until well combined.

5. Add the flour to the mixture and whisk until just combined.

6. Pour the batter into the prepared ramekins, filling each one about 3/4 full.

7. Bake for 12-14 minutes, or until the edges are set and the center is still slightly jiggly.

8. Remove from the oven and let cool for 5 minutes.

9. Run a knife around the edges of the ramekins to loosen the cakes, then invert them onto serving plates.

10. Serve the cakes warm, garnished with a sprinkle of sea salt and ground long pepper.

This long pepper and sea salt molten chocolate cake recipe is an easy and original twist on the classic molten chocolate cake. The long pepper adds a unique spice to the cake, while the sea salt enhances the sweetness of the chocolate.

The cake is perfect for a special occasion or a cozy night in.

V

Culinary Adventures

Drawing inspiration from the vibrant tapestry of medieval cuisine, we'll explore the rich and diverse flavors, aromas, and techniques that once graced the tables of knights and kings. Through a creative lens, we'll reinterpret age-old recipes and timeless ingredient combinations, infusing them with a touch of modern flair. As we embark on this culinary voyage, we honor the wisdom of the past while embracing the flavors of the present, resulting in a harmonious fusion of traditions that redefines the art of gastronomy.

In this Section, we will work with the flavour profiles and ingredients typical of Medieval Europe to recreate traditional dishes and create contemporary recipes that echo the past.

The Spice Game, 11th to the 15th centuries

Medieval spices held a mesmerizing allure that transcended their culinary value, becoming symbols of wealth, power, and exoticism. These precious commodities were not just ingredients; they were treasured luxuries that could transform bland medieval fare into a flavorful extravaganza. One little-known fact about these coveted spices is that their scarcity and high prices during the Middle Ages often led to elaborate schemes to counterfeit or adulterate them. For instance, saffron, one of the most expensive spices, was frequently replaced with cheaper alternatives like safflower or even marigold petals.

Spices and Flavor Profile in the Middle Ages

Spices were an essential part of medieval cuisine and were used for culinary, medicinal, and cosmetic purposes. The use of spices in medieval Europe was influenced by the trade routes that brought them from the East, and the spices were considered a luxury item due to their high cost and rarity. The most common spices and flavor profiles that were used in medieval Europe?

1. Cinnamon: Cinnamon was one of the most popular spices in medieval Europe and was used in both sweet and savory dishes. It was believed to have medicinal properties and was used to treat various ailments.

2. Clove: Clove was another popular spice in medieval Europe and was used in both food and medicine. It was believed to have antiseptic properties and was used to treat toothaches and other dental problems.

3. Nutmeg: Nutmeg was a highly prized spice in medieval Europe and was used in both sweet and savory dishes. It was believed to have medicinal properties and was used to treat digestive problems.

4. Ginger: Ginger was a popular spice in medieval Europe and was used in both food and medicine. It was believed to have anti-inflammatory properties and was used to treat various ailments.

5. Pepper: Pepper was a common spice in medieval Europe and was used in both food and medicine. It was believed to have digestive properties and was used to treat various digestive problems.

6. Saffron: Saffron was a highly prized spice in medieval Europe and was used in both sweet and savory dishes. It was believed to have medicinal properties and was used to treat various ailments.

The flavor profile of medieval cuisine was characterized by a combination of sweet and sour flavors, which were achieved by using spices such as verjuice, wine, and vinegar in combination with spices such as black pepper, saffron, and ginger. Honey or sugar was also used to give dishes a sweet-sour flavor.

The use of spices in medieval cuisine differed from contemporary European and American flavor profiles in that medieval cuisine relied heavily on the use of spices to flavor dishes, while contemporary cuisine relies more on the use of herbs and other flavorings. Additionally, contemporary cuisine tends to use fewer spices and relies more on the natural flavors of the ingredients. The use of spices in medieval cuisine was also influenced by the trade routes that brought them from the East, while contemporary cuisine has access to a wider variety of spices from around the world.

Let's start with an elevated example of this flavour profile.

Medieval Spiced Chicken with Vinegar and Gold Flakes

Ingredients

- 4 chicken breasts, boneless and skinless
- 1 tbsp olive oil
- 1 large onion, chopped
- 2 cloves garlic, minced
- 2 carrots, peeled and chopped
- 2 stalks celery, chopped
- 1 bay leaf
- 1/2 tsp dried thyme
- 1/2 tsp dried marjoram
- 1/2 tsp dried rosemary
- 1/2 tsp salt
- 1/4 tsp black pepper
- 1/4 tsp ground coriander
- 1/4 tsp ground cumin
- 1/4 tsp ground ginger
- 1/4 tsp ground cinnamon
- 1/4 tsp ground cloves
- 1/4 cup red wine vinegar
- Gold flakes, for garnish

Instructions

1. Preheat the oven to 375°F.
2. In a large skillet, heat the olive oil over medium heat.
3. Add the chopped onion, minced garlic, chopped carrots, and chopped celery and sauté until the vegetables are tender.
4. Add the bay leaf, dried thyme, dried marjoram, dried rosemary, salt, black pepper, ground coriander, ground cumin, ground ginger, ground cinnamon, and ground cloves.
5. Sauté the spices for 1-2 minutes or until fragrant.
6. Add the red wine vinegar and stir to combine.
7. Remove the skillet from the heat.
8. Place the chicken breasts in a baking dish and pour the spiced vinegar mixture over the chicken.
9. Cover the baking dish with foil and bake for 25-30 minutes or until the chicken is cooked through.
10. Remove the foil and bake for an additional 5-10 minutes or until the chicken is golden brown.
11. Remove the chicken from the oven and let it rest for 5 minutes.
12. Garnish with gold flakes before serving.

Practical Examples: Culinary Uses of Plants in Medieval Gardens

Medieval gardens were not only a source of beauty and pleasure, but also a source of food and medicine. Once you have your list of edible plants growing in your personal medieval garden and you are familiar with the flavour and spice profiles that were typical of the Age, you will be well suited to recreate historic dishes, or experiment with a full range of ingredients and flavours presented by your pantry, garden and historic research. You do not need a culinary education or experience working on the line. You do need some time and a willingness to try something new with somethings old.

Here are 20 examples of plants commonly found in medieval gardens and their culinary uses:

1. Cabbages
Culinary uses: Cabbage soup, cabbage rolls, coleslaw
Recipe: Medieval Cabbage Soup

2. Carrots
Culinary uses: Carrot pudding, carrot salad, roasted carrots
Recipe: Medieval Carrot Pudding

3. Leeks
Culinary uses: Leek soup, leek tart, leek and potato pie
Recipe: Medieval Leek Tart

4. Onions
Culinary uses: Onion soup, onion tart, onion quiche
Recipe: Medieval Onion Tart and Medieval Onion and Pear Pottage with Medieval-style Biscuits:

5. Peas
Culinary uses: Pea soup, pea and ham pie, pea risotto
Recipe: Medieval Pea Soup

6. Beans
Culinary uses: Bean soup, bean stew, bean salad
Recipe: Medieval Bean Stew

7. Radishes
Culinary uses: Radish salad, radish sandwich, pickled radishes
Recipe: Medieval Radish Salad

8. Turnips
Culinary uses: Turnip soup, roasted turnips, mashed turnips
Recipe: Medieval Turnip Soup

9. Apples
Culinary uses: Apple pie, apple tart, baked apples
Recipe: Medieval Apple Tart

10. Pears
Culinary uses: Pear tart, poached pears, pear and almond cake
Recipe: Medieval pear poached in hypocras

11. Plums
Culinary uses: Plum pudding, plum tart, plum cake
Recipe: Medieval Plums roasted in honey

12. Cherries
Culinary uses: Cherry pie, cherry tart, cherry clafoutis
Recipe: Medieval Honey stewed cherries on medieval sweet bread

13. Grapes
Culinary uses: Grape tart, grape jelly, grape juice
Recipe: Pork in Grapes and Drunken Pork with Grapes

14. Figs
Culinary uses: Fig tart, fig jam, fig and almond cake
Recipes: Spiced Fig and Honey Compote and Stuffed Figs with Medieval Spices

15. Olives
Culinary uses: Olive tapenade, marinated olives, olive bread
Recipe: Medieval Olive and Fig salad

16. Quinces
Culinary uses: Quince jelly, quince paste, quince tart
Recipe: Medieval Spiced sausages with Quince paste Sauce on mashed sweet potatoes

17. Melons
Culinary uses: Melon salad, melon sorbet, melon jam
Recipe: Medieval Flavoured Melon and Anchovy Appetizer

18. Acorn Squash
Culinary uses: soup, pies roasted
Recipe: Acorn Squash Ice Cream with Medieval Spiced Chocolate Syrup

20. Orache
Culinary uses: salads, soups and stews.
Recipe: Orache Soup with Cream Dollop and Saffron

Medieval Cabbage Soup Recipe

Medieval cabbage soup, also known as "pottage," was a staple dish for peasants in the Middle Ages. One interesting fact about this humble meal is that it often included a variety of ingredients beyond just cabbage. Medieval cooks would make use of whatever vegetables were available, such as turnips, carrots, leeks, and even wild greens. Additionally, they would add grains like barley or oats to thicken the soup and make it more filling. The use of various herbs and spices was also common to enhance the flavor. This adaptable and frugal approach to cooking reflected the resourcefulness of medieval cooks in making the most of their limited ingredients, resulting in a hearty and nourishing dish that sustained many throughout this historical era.

Ingredients

- 1 small cabbage, chopped
- 1 onion, chopped
- 2 cloves garlic, minced
- 2 tbsp butter
- 1 quart chicken or vegetable broth
- 1 tsp salt
- 1/4 tsp black pepper
- 1/4 tsp ground coriander
- 1/4 tsp ground cinnamon
- 1/4 tsp sugar
- 1/4 tsp saffron strands
- 1/2 cup barley

Instructions

1. In a large pot, melt the butter over medium heat.
2. Add the chopped onion and minced garlic and sauté until the onion is translucent.
3. Add the chopped cabbage and sauté for 5-7 minutes or until the cabbage is slightly softened.
4. Add the chicken or vegetable broth, salt, black pepper, coriander, cinnamon, sugar, and saffron strands.
5. Bring the soup to a boil, then reduce the heat and simmer for 30 minutes.
6. Add the barley to the soup and continue to simmer for an additional 30 minutes or until the barley is tender.
7. Serve hot.

Medieval Carrot Pudding Recipe with a Spicy Twist

In medieval Europe, puddings were quite different from what we think of today. They were often savory dishes rather than sweet desserts. One notable fact is that carrots were a common ingredient in medieval puddings. Carrot pudding, made by combining grated or mashed carrots with other ingredients like breadcrumbs, eggs, and spices, was a popular dish during this time. These puddings were typically seasoned with spices like cinnamon, nutmeg, and cloves, reflecting the medieval preference for combining sweet and savory flavors in their cuisine. This culinary tradition illustrates how the use of vegetables, like carrots, was versatile in medieval cooking, appearing in both savory and sweet preparations.

Ingredients:
- 1 lb carrots, peeled and grated
- 1/2 cup unsalted butter, softened
- 1/2 cup brown sugar
- 1/2 cup all-purpose flour
- 1/2 tsp baking powder
- 1/2 tsp cinnamon
- 1/4 tsp nutmeg
- 1/4 tsp salt
- 2 eggs, beaten
- 1/2 cup raisins
- 1/4 cup chopped walnuts
- 1/4 tsp ground ginger
- 1/4 tsp ground cloves
- 1/4 tsp ground cardamom

Instructions:
1. Preheat the oven to 350°F.
2. In a large mixing bowl, cream together the butter and brown sugar until light and fluffy.
3. In a separate bowl, whisk together the flour, baking powder, cinnamon, nutmeg, salt, ginger, cloves, and cardamom.
4. Add the dry ingredients to the butter mixture and mix until well combined.
5. Stir in the grated carrots, beaten eggs, raisins, and chopped walnuts.
6. Pour the mixture into a greased 9-inch baking dish.
7. Bake for 45-50 minutes or until a toothpick inserted into the center comes out clean.
8. Let the pudding cool for 10-15 minutes before serving.

Medieval Leek Tart Recipe

Medieval leek tart, also known as "leek and cheese pie," was a savory dish enjoyed during the Middle Ages. Leeks were a common vegetable in medieval European cuisine, appreciated for their mild flavor and suitability for various dishes. To prepare a medieval leek tart, cooks would typically chop and sauté leeks until tender and mix them with ingredients like cheese, eggs, and various herbs and spices. This mixture would then be enclosed in a pastry crust made from a simple mixture of flour and water. The result was a hearty and flavorful tart, enjoyed by both the nobility and commoners of the time.

Ingredients
   * For the crust
- 2 cups all-purpose flour
- 1/2 teaspoon salt
- 7 tablespoons unsalted butter, chilled and cut into pieces
- 3 tablespoons ice water

   * For the filling
- 4 leeks, white and light green parts only, thinly sliced
- 2 tablespoons unsalted butter
- 1/2 teaspoon salt
- 1/4 teaspoon black pepper
- 1/4 teaspoon ground nutmeg
- 1/2 cup heavy cream
- 2 eggs, beaten
- 1/2 cup grated Parmesan cheese

Instructions
1. Preheat the oven to 375°F.
2. In a large mixing bowl, whisk together the flour and salt.
3. Add the chilled butter and use a pastry cutter or your fingers to work the butter into the flour until the mixture resembles coarse crumbs.
4. Add the ice water and mix until the dough comes together.
5. Roll out the dough on a floured surface and transfer it to a 9-inch tart pan.
6. Trim the edges and prick the bottom of the crust with a fork.
7. Bake the crust for 10-12 minutes or until lightly golden.
8. In a large skillet, melt the butter over medium heat.
9. Add the sliced leeks and sauté until tender, about 10 minutes.
10. Season the leeks with salt, black pepper, and nutmeg.
11. In a mixing bowl, whisk together the heavy cream and beaten eggs.
12. Add the grated Parmesan cheese and mix well.
13. Spread the sautéed leeks evenly over the pre-baked crust.
14. Pour the egg and cream mixture over the leeks.
15. Bake the tart for 25-30 minutes or until the filling is set and golden brown.
16. Let the tart cool for 10-15 minutes before serving.

French Onion Tart Recipe

The medieval French onion tart, known as "Tarte à l'Oignon," was a savory delicacy that has evolved into the modern-day French Onion Tart or "Tarte à l'Oignon Gratinée." During medieval times, this dish was simpler and had a different preparation method than its contemporary counterpart. It featured a basic pastry crust filled with a mixture of caramelized onions, cream, and seasonings, which were then baked to perfection.

Ingredients
  *For the crust
- 1 1/4 cups all-purpose flour
- 1/4 tsp kosher salt
- 1/2 cup unsalted butter, chilled and cubed
- 1/4 cup ice water

  *For the filling
- 2 large onions, thinly sliced
- 2 tbsp unsalted butter
- 1/4 tsp kosher salt
- 1/4 tsp black pepper
- 1/4 tsp dried thyme
- 1/4 cup heavy cream
- 2 eggs, beaten
- 1/2 cup grated Gruyere cheese

Instructions
1. Preheat the oven to 375°F.
2. In a large mixing bowl, whisk together the flour and salt.
3. Add the chilled butter and use a pastry cutter or your fingers to work the butter into the flour until the mixture resembles coarse crumbs.
4. Add the ice water and mix until the dough comes together.
5. Roll out the dough on a floured surface and transfer it to a 9-inch tart pan.
6. Trim the edges and prick the bottom of the crust with a fork.
7. Bake the crust for 10-12 minutes or until lightly golden.
8. In a large skillet, melt the butter over medium heat.
9. Add the sliced onions and sauté until tender and caramelized, about 20-25 minutes.
10. Season the onions with salt, black pepper, and dried thyme.
11. In a mixing bowl, whisk together the heavy cream and beaten eggs.
12. Add the grated Gruyere cheese and mix well.
13. Spread the caramelized onions evenly over the pre-baked crust.
14. Pour the egg and cream mixture over the onions.
15. Bake the tart for 25-30 minutes or until the filling is set and golden brown.
16. Let the tart cool for 10-15 minutes before serving.

English Onion Tart Recipe

One interesting aspect of the English onion tart is its versatility. While the basic ingredients remain consistent, there can be regional variations and personal touches in terms of the choice of pastry, seasonings, or additional ingredients like cheese or herbs. The result is a comforting and flavorful dish that has remained a favorite in English cuisine, often served as a main course or as part of a hearty meal.

Ingredients

*** For the crust**
- 1 1/4 cups all-purpose flour
- 1/4 tsp kosher salt
- 1/2 cup unsalted butter, chilled and cubed
- 1/4 cup ice water

*** For the filling**
- 2 large onions, thinly sliced
- 2 tbsp unsalted butter
- 1/4 tsp kosher salt
- 1/4 tsp black pepper
- 1/4 tsp dried sage
- 1/4 cup heavy cream
- 2 eggs, beaten
- 1/2 cup grated Cheddar cheese

Instructions

1. Preheat the oven to 375°F.
2. In a large mixing bowl, whisk together the flour and salt.
3. Add the chilled butter and use a pastry cutter or your fingers to work the butter into the flour until the mixture resembles coarse crumbs.
4. Add the ice water and mix until the dough comes together.
5. Roll out the dough on a floured surface and transfer it to a 9-inch tart pan.
6. Trim the edges and prick the bottom of the crust with a fork.
7. Bake the crust for 10-12 minutes or until lightly golden.
8. In a large skillet, melt the butter over medium heat.
9. Add the sliced onions and sauté until tender and caramelized, about 20-25 minutes.
10. Season the onions with salt, black pepper, and dried sage.
11. In a mixing bowl, whisk together the heavy cream and beaten eggs.
12. Add the grated Cheddar cheese and mix well.
13. Spread the caramelized onions evenly over the pre-baked crust.
14. Pour the egg and cream mixture over the onions.
15. Bake the tart for 25-30 minutes or until the filling is set and golden brown.
16. Let the tart cool for 10-15 minutes before serving.

Medieval Onion and Pear Pottage

Medieval onion and pear pottage was a unique and flavorful dish that combined the sweetness of pears with the savory taste of onions, creating a balance of flavors that was characteristic of medieval cuisine.

To prepare this pottage, onions were typically sliced and sautéed until they became tender and slightly caramelized. Then, ripe pears were peeled, cored, and added to the onions. The mixture was cooked together with broth or water, and sometimes flavored with herbs and spices such as cinnamon or nutmeg.

The result was a hearty and sweet-savory stew-like dish that showcased the medieval appreciation for blending contrasting flavors in their recipes. Onion and pear pottage is a fascinating example of the creative and unexpected combinations that were enjoyed during that era.

Ingredients

- 2 tablespoons butter
- 2 onions, chopped
- 2 pears, peeled and chopped
- 4 cups vegetable broth
- 1/2 teaspoon ground cinnamon
- 1/4 teaspoon ground nutmeg
- Salt and pepper to taste

Instructions

1. In a large pot, melt the butter over medium heat.
2. Add the chopped onions and sauté until they are translucent.
3. Add the chopped pears to the pot and stir to combine.
4. Pour in the vegetable broth and bring the mixture to a boil.
5. Reduce the heat to low and simmer for 20-25 minutes, or until the pears are tender.
6. Remove the pot from the heat and let it cool slightly.
7. Using an immersion blender, puree the soup until smooth.
8. Return the soup to the pot and stir in the ground cinnamon, ground nutmeg, salt, and pepper.
9. Allow the soup to simmer for another 5-10 minutes to let the flavours meld together.

Medieval-Style Biscuits

Medieval-style biscuits, also known as "biscuit" in Middle English, were quite different from the modern, sweet, and crunchy biscuits we are familiar with today. In medieval times, biscuits were more akin to a form of bread, often hard and long-lasting, suitable for travelers and soldiers. Here, we are serving them with the Medieval onion and pear pottage, but you can use them for a lot more creative purposes.

Medieval biscuits were not commonly added directly to stews as we might think of today with dumplings. Instead, the biscuits of that era were often consumed separately from the stew or used as a type of bread to accompany the meal.

Medieval biscuits, sometimes referred to as "hard tack," "ship's biscuit," or "rusks," were extremely dry and hard. They were made to have a long shelf life and were popular among travelers, soldiers, and sailors because they could be carried on journeys without spoiling. These biscuits were typically dipped into liquids like wine or ale to soften them and add flavor.

Ingredients
- 2 cups all-purpose flour
- 1/2 teaspoon salt
- 1/2 teaspoon baking powder
- 1/2 cup unsalted butter, chilled and cubed
- 1/2 cup milk
- 1 tablespoon honey

Instructions
1. Preheat the oven to 375°F (190°C).
2. In a large bowl, whisk together the flour, salt, and baking powder.
3. Add the cubed butter to the bowl and use a pastry cutter or your fingers to cut the butter into the flour mixture until it resembles coarse crumbs.
4. In a small bowl, whisk together the milk and honey.
5. Add the milk mixture to the flour mixture and stir until a dough forms.
6. Turn the dough out onto a floured surface and knead it gently.
7. Roll the dough out to 1/2-inch thickness and cut it into rounds using a biscuit cutter.
8. Place the biscuits on a baking sheet lined with parchment paper.
9. Bake the biscuits for 15-20 minutes, or until they are golden brown.

To serve, ladle the Medieval Onion and Pear Pottage into bowls and serve with the Medieval-style Biscuits on the side. Enjoy this hearty and flavourful meal that combines the sweetness of pears with the savoury flavour of onions.

French Medieval Pea Soup Recipe

French medieval pea soup, known as "Soupe aux Pois," was a staple in the diets of people during the Middle Ages in France. Peas were a common crop in medieval France and other parts of Europe. They were easily dried and stored, making them a valuable source of nutrition during the winter months.

Medieval pea soup was made with basic ingredients like dried peas, water or broth, and often included vegetables like onions, leeks, or carrots. Meat or bones might be added for flavor, but this depended on one's social status and availability of resources.

Pea soup has also appeared in literature and folklore, such as in Victor Hugo's "Les Misérables," where it is associated with poverty and hardship.

Ingredients:
- 1 1/2 cups dry split peas, sorted and rinsed
- 4 cups (1 quart) water
- 3 tablespoons olive oil
- 1 large onion, chopped
- 2 cloves garlic, minced
- 2 carrots, peeled and chopped
- 2 stalks celery, chopped
- 1 bay leaf
- 1/2 tsp dried thyme
- 1/2 tsp dried marjoram
- 1/2 tsp dried rosemary
- 1/2 tsp salt
- 1/4 tsp black pepper
- 1/4 tsp ground coriander
- 1/4 tsp ground cumin
- 1/4 tsp ground ginger

Instructions
1. In a large pot, combine the split peas and water and bring to a boil.
2. Reduce the heat and simmer for 30 minutes or until the peas are tender.
3. In a separate pan, heat the olive oil over medium heat.
4. Add the chopped onion, minced garlic, chopped carrots, and chopped celery and sauté until the vegetables are tender.
5. Add the sautéed vegetables to the pot with the split peas.
6. Add the bay leaf, dried thyme, dried marjoram, dried rosemary, salt, black pepper, ground coriander, ground cumin, and ground ginger.
7. Simmer the soup for an additional 10-15 minutes or until the flavors have melded together.
8. Remove the bay leaf and serve hot.

English Medieval Pea Soup Recipe

Medieval English pea soup, often referred to as "Pease Pottage," was a hearty and staple dish during the Middle Ages in England. This soup had the advantage of being a reliable source of nutrition during harsh winters when fresh vegetables were scarce. Its long shelf life made it valuable for survival.

Pease pottage has appeared in English literature and folklore, such as in the nursery rhyme "Pease Porridge Hot," which reflects its popularity and cultural significance.

Ingredients

- 1 lb dried split peas, sorted and rinsed
- 8 cups (2 quarts) water
- 2 tbsp unsalted butter
- 1 large onion, chopped
- 2 cloves garlic, minced
- 2 carrots, peeled and chopped
- 2 stalks celery, chopped
- 1 bay leaf
- 1/2 tsp dried thyme
- 1/2 tsp dried marjoram
- 1/2 tsp dried rosemary
- 1/2 tsp salt
- 1/4 tsp black pepper
- 1/4 tsp ground nutmeg
- 1/4 tsp ground cloves

Instructions
1. In a large pot, combine the split peas and water and bring to a boil.
2. Reduce the heat and simmer for 30 minutes or until the peas are tender.
3. In a separate pan, melt the butter over medium heat.
4. Add the chopped onion, minced garlic, chopped carrots, and chopped celery and sauté until the vegetables are tender.
5. Add the sautéed vegetables to the pot with the split peas.
6. Add the bay leaf, dried thyme, dried marjoram, dried rosemary, salt, black pepper, ground nutmeg, and ground cloves.
7. Simmer the soup for an additional 10-15 minutes or until the flavors have melded together.
8. Remove the bay leaf and serve hot.

Medieval Bean Stew with a Raisins and Walnuts

One intriguing aspect of this dish was the combination of sweet and savory flavors. The raisins added a natural sweetness to the stew, while the walnuts provided a satisfying crunch and nutty taste. The inclusion of spices and herbs like cinnamon, cloves, or sage enhanced the overall flavor profile, creating a complex and well-balanced taste.

Ingredients

- 2 cups dried beans, soaked overnight
- 6 cups water
- 1 tbsp olive oil
- 1 large onion, chopped
- 2 cloves garlic, minced
- 2 carrots, peeled and chopped
- 2 stalks celery, chopped
- 1 bay leaf
- 1/2 tsp dried thyme
- 1/2 tsp dried marjoram
- 1/2 tsp dried rosemary
- 1/2 tsp salt
- 1/4 tsp black pepper
- 1/4 tsp ground coriander
- 1/4 tsp ground cumin
- 1/4 tsp ground ginger
- 1/4 tsp ground cinnamon
- 1/4 tsp ground cloves
- 1/4 cup red wine vinegar
- 1/4 cup honey
- 1/4 cup gold raisins
- 1/4 cup chopped walnuts
- Gold flakes, for garnish

Instructions

1. In a large pot, combine the soaked beans and water and bring to a boil.
2. Reduce the heat and simmer for 1-2 hours or until the beans are tender.
3. In a separate pan, heat the olive oil over medium heat.
4. Add the chopped onion, minced garlic, chopped carrots, and chopped celery and sauté until the vegetables are tender.
5. Add the bay leaf, dried thyme, dried marjoram, dried rosemary, salt, black pepper, ground coriander, ground cumin, ground ginger, ground cinnamon, and ground cloves.
6. Sauté the spices for 1-2 minutes or until fragrant.
7. Add the spiced vegetables to the pot with the cooked beans.
8. Add the red wine vinegar, honey, gold raisins, and chopped walnuts.
9. Simmer the stew for an additional 10-15 minutes or until the flavors have melded together.
10. Remove the bay leaf and serve hot.
11. Garnish with gold flakes before serving.

Medieval Radish Salad, Three Ways

A fascinating fact about radishes in medieval times is that they were believed to have certain aphrodisiac properties. Radishes were associated with fertility and were thought to increase sexual desire. This belief led to radishes being included in various love potions and recipes designed to enhance romantic relationships.

In medieval folklore and herbal medicine, radishes were sometimes considered a symbol of passion and were thought to have the power to stimulate desire. While these notions may seem quaint or superstitious today, they provide insight into the cultural and symbolic significance of food during the Middle Ages, where even everyday vegetables like radishes could be imbued with romantic and mystical connotations.

Recipe 1: Medieval Radish Salad with Fennel

Ingredients

- 1 bunch radishes, thinly sliced
- 1 bulb fennel, thinly sliced
- 1/4 cup chopped fresh parsley
- 1/4 cup chopped fresh chives
- 1/4 cup chopped walnuts
- 1/4 cup crumbled gorgonzola cheese
- 2 tablespoons red wine vinegar
- 2 tablespoons olive oil
- Salt and pepper to taste

Instructions

1. In a large bowl, combine the radishes, fennel, parsley, chives, walnuts, and gorgonzola cheese.
2. In a small bowl, whisk together the red wine vinegar, olive oil, salt, and pepper to make the dressing.
3. Pour the dressing over the vegetables and toss to combine.
4. Serve immediately.

Recipe 2: Medieval Radish Salad with Honey Dijon Dressing

Ingredients

- 1 bunch radishes, thinly sliced
- 1/4 cup chopped fresh parsley
- 1/4 cup chopped fresh chives
- 1/4 cup chopped walnuts
- 2 tablespoons red wine vinegar

- 2 tablespoons honey
- 1 tablespoon dijon mustard
- 1/4 teaspoon ground cinnamon
- 1/4 teaspoon ground cloves
- 1/4 teaspoon ground nutmeg
- 1/4 cup olive oil
- Salt and pepper to taste

Instructions
1. In a large bowl, combine the radishes, parsley, chives, and walnuts.
2. In a small bowl, whisk together the red wine vinegar, honey, dijon mustard, cinnamon, cloves, nutmeg, olive oil, salt, and pepper to make the dressing.
3. Pour the dressing over the vegetables and toss to combine.
4. Serve immediately.

Both of these recipes are inspired by medieval cuisine, which often featured simple, fresh ingredients and bold flavors. The radishes add a crisp, refreshing crunch to the salads, while the fennel or complex dressing provides a unique and flavorful twist. These salads would be perfect as a light lunch or as a side dish for a larger meal. Enjoy!

Recipe 3: Medieval Radish Salad with Seafood

The medieval European diet was heavily influenced by what was readily available. Inland regions relied more on freshwater fish, game, and domesticated livestock for their protein sources.

Seafood, including shrimp and crab, was often considered a luxury item in medieval Europe. It was expensive and mainly accessible to the upper classes who could afford the cost of transportation from coastal areas. So, let's call this a royal dish.

Ingredients

- 1 pound cooked shrimp or crabmeat
- 1 bunch radishes, thinly sliced
- 1/4 cup chopped fresh parsley
- 1/4 cup olive oil
- 2 tablespoons red wine vinegar
- Salt and pepper to taste

Instructions
1. In a large bowl, combine the cooked seafood, radishes, and parsley.
2. In a small bowl, whisk together the olive oil, red wine vinegar, salt, and pepper.
3. Pour the dressing over the seafood and vegetables and toss to combine.
4. Serve immediately.

German Medieval Turnip Soup

German medieval turnip soup, known as "Rübeneintopf" in German, was a hearty and nourishing dish commonly enjoyed during the Middle Ages in Germany.

Turnips were particularly important in northern European countries like Germany because they could be stored through the winter. This made them a valuable source of sustenance during the colder months when fresh produce was scarce.

Rübeneintopf is a dish with numerous regional variations in Germany. Each region had its own way of preparing the stew, often incorporating locally available ingredients.

Ingredients

- 600g turnips, peeled and chopped
- 400g pork belly, chopped
- 2 eggs
- Aged pecorino cheese
- Goat milk
- Black pepper
- Saffron
- Salt

Instructions

1. In a large pot, cook the pork belly until browned and crispy.
2. Add the chopped turnips to the pot and cook for a few minutes until they start to soften.
3. Add enough water to the pot to cover the turnips and pork belly.
4. Bring the water to a boil and then reduce the heat to a simmer.
5. Simmer the soup for about 30 minutes, or until the turnips are soft and tender.
6. In a small bowl, whisk together the eggs, pecorino cheese, goat milk, black pepper, saffron, and salt.
7. Slowly pour the egg mixture into the soup, stirring constantly.
8. Continue to cook the soup for a few more minutes until the egg mixture is cooked through.
9. Serve the soup hot, garnished with additional black pepper and saffron if desired.

This recipe is a delicious and hearty soup that would have been enjoyed in the Middle Ages. The turnips provide a sweet and earthy flavor, while the pork belly adds richness and depth. The egg and cheese mixture adds a creamy texture and a complex flavor profile. This soup is perfect for a cold winter day and is sure to warm you up from the inside out. Enjoy!

Spiced Apple and Honey Tart

Medieval cuisine was known for its extensive use of spices. Spiced apple tarts were no exception, often featuring a blend of cinnamon, nutmeg, cloves, and other spices. These spices were highly prized for their exotic flavors and were a symbol of wealth and sophistication.

Medieval spiced apple tarts sometimes incorporated savory elements like cheese or minced meat alongside the sweet apples and spices. This combination of sweet and savory was a common feature of medieval dishes.

The crust of medieval apple tarts could vary. Some were made with a basic pastry dough, while others used a breadcrumb or ground almond base. The choice of crust often depended on availability and regional preferences.

Spiced apple tarts were considered a luxurious dessert in medieval times. The availability of ingredients like apples, sugar, and spices made them relatively expensive, so they were often enjoyed by the nobility and wealthy.

Ingredients

- 1 pre-made pie crust
- 4 medium apples, peeled and thinly sliced
- 1/4 cup honey
- 1/4 cup brown sugar
- 1 tablespoon cinnamon
- 1/2 teaspoon nutmeg
- 1/4 teaspoon cloves
- 1/4 teaspoon ginger
- 1/4 teaspoon salt
- 1/4 cup butter, melted

Instructions

1. Preheat the oven to 375°F.
2. Roll out the pie crust and place it in a 9-inch tart pan.
3. In a large bowl, mix together the sliced apples, honey, brown sugar, cinnamon, nutmeg, cloves, ginger, and salt.
4. Pour the apple mixture into the pie crust.
5. Drizzle the melted butter over the top of the apple mixture.
6. Bake the tart for 45-50 minutes, or until the crust is golden brown and the apples are tender.
7. Serve the tart warm, garnished with a dollop of whipped cream or a scoop of vanilla ice cream.

A Savory Apple Tart with a Medieval Flavor Profile and a Wine Sauce

This savory apple tart is a delicious and unique take on a classic dessert. The blue cheese and walnuts add a savory and nutty flavor, while the wine sauce provides a sweet and tangy contrast. The medieval flavor profile is enhanced by the addition of dried apricots and warm spices. This tart would be perfect as a main course for a fall dinner party or as a unique addition to a holiday meal.

Ingredients

* **For the Tart:**
- 1 premade pie crust
- 4 medium apples, peeled and thinly sliced
- 1 cup crumbled blue cheese
- 1/4 cup chopped walnuts
- 1/4 cup chopped fresh parsley
- 1 tablespoon olive oil
- 1/4 teaspoon salt
- 1/4 teaspoon black pepper
- 1/4 teaspoon dried thyme

* **For the Wine Sauce:**
- 1 cup red wine
- 1/2 cup chicken or vegetable broth
- 1/4 cup honey
- 1/4 cup chopped dried apricots
- 1/4 teaspoon ground cinnamon
- 1/4 teaspoon ground cloves
- 1/4 teaspoon ground nutmeg
- Salt and pepper to taste

Instructions
1. Preheat the oven to 375°F.
2. Roll out the pie crust and place it in a 9inch tart pan.
3. In a large bowl, mix together the sliced apples, blue cheese, walnuts, parsley, olive oil, salt, black pepper, and thyme.
4. Pour the apple mixture into the pie crust.
5. Bake the tart for 45-50 minutes, or until the crust is golden brown and the apples are tender.
6. While the tart is baking, prepare the wine sauce.
7. In a small saucepan, combine the red wine, broth, honey, dried apricots, cinnamon, cloves, nutmeg, salt, and pepper.
8. Bring the mixture to a boil and then reduce the heat to a simmer.
9. Simmer the sauce for about 20-25 minutes, or until it has thickened and reduced by about half.
10. Serve the tart warm, garnished with additional chopped parsley and drizzled with the wine sauce.

Medieval Pear Poached in Hypocras and Spiced with Pepper
with a recipe for homemade hypocras included

Pears held symbolic meaning in medieval Europe. They were associated with prosperity, abundance, and happiness. Pears could often be found in medieval art and literature as symbols of good fortune and wealth. This Medieval Pear Poached in Hypocras and Spiced with Pepper is a unique and flavorful dessert that is perfect for a special occasion. The homemade hypocras adds a warm and spicy flavor to the pears, while the black peppercorns provide a subtle heat. This recipe is easy to make and is sure to impress your guests. Enjoy!

Ingredients

* For the Hypocras:
- 1 bottle of red wine
- 1/2 cup honey
- 1 cinnamon stick
- 1 star anise
- 1 cardamom pod
- 1/4 teaspoon allspice
- 1/4 teaspoon black peppercorns
- 1/4 teaspoon ground ginger

* For the Poached Pears:
- 4 medium pears, peeled and cored
- 2 cups hypocras
- 1/4 cup honey
- 1 cinnamon stick
- 1/4 teaspoon black peppercorns

Instructions
1. To make the hypocras, combine the red wine, honey, cinnamon stick, star anise, cardamom pod, allspice, black peppercorns, and ground ginger in a large pot.
2. Bring the mixture to a boil and then reduce the heat to a simmer.
3. Simmer the hypocras for about 2025 minutes, or until the flavors have melded together.
4. Strain the hypocras through a fine mesh strainer and discard the solids.
5. To make the poached pears, combine the hypocras, honey, cinnamon stick, and black peppercorns in a large pot.
6. Bring the mixture to a boil and then reduce the heat to a simmer.
7. Add the pears to the pot and simmer for about 2025 minutes, or until the pears are tender.
8. Remove the pears from the pot and set them aside.
9. Increase the heat to high and boil the poaching liquid until it has reduced by about half and has thickened into a syrup.
10. Serve the poached pears warm, drizzled with the syrup and garnished with additional black peppercorns.

Hypocras

Hypocras is a spiced wine that was popular in medieval Europe. It was made by mixing wine with sugar, cinnamon, ginger, and other spices. Here are some key points about hypocras:

- Hypocras was a popular drink in medieval Europe, and it was often consumed for both medicinal and culinary purposes.

- The name "hypocras" comes from the Latin "vīnum Hippocraticum," which means "Hippocratic wine." It was named after the Greek physician Hippocrates, who was known for his medical writings and teachings.

- Hypocras was made by mixing wine with sugar and spices, usually including cinnamon, ginger, and cloves. The mixture was then heated and allowed to steep for several hours.

- Hypocras was believed to have medicinal properties and was often used to treat a variety of ailments, including digestive issues and respiratory problems.

- Hypocras was also used as a culinary ingredient and was often added to sauces, stews, and other dishes to add flavor and depth.

- Hypocras fell out of favor in the 19th century but has recently seen a resurgence in popularity among modern foodies and historians.

Hypocras is a unique and flavorful drink that has a rich history and legacy in medieval Europe that deserves to be reincorporated into the contemporary pantry and culinary practice. It was a versatile beverage that was consumed for both medicinal and culinary purposes and was often made with a variety of spices and sweeteners.

Renaissance Elixir

Let's jump forward a few centuries and play with Hypocras. This Renaissance Elixir is a modern take on the historical Hypocras, blending the flavors of red wine, spiced syrup, and brandy with a touch of citrus and bitters. It's a sophisticated and aromatic cocktail that pays homage to the past while offering a unique and delightful drinking experience.

Ingredients

- 2 oz red wine (ideally a bold red like Cabernet Sauvignon)
- 1/2 oz brandy
- 1/2 oz Hypocras syrup (see instructions below)
- 1/2 oz fresh orange juice
- 1 dash aromatic bitters (Angostura or similar)
- Orange twist, for garnish

   * For the Hypocras Syrup:
- 1 cup red wine
- 1/2 cup honey
- 2 cinnamon sticks
- 45 cloves
- Zest of one orange
- Zest of one lemon
- 1 star anise pod

Instructions

1. Start by preparing the Hypocras syrup. In a saucepan, combine the red wine, honey, cinnamon sticks, cloves, orange zest, lemon zest, and star anise. Heat over low heat, stirring until the honey is dissolved.

2. Simmer the mixture gently for about 1015 minutes, allowing the flavors to meld and the syrup to reduce slightly. Remove from heat and let it cool.

3. Once cooled, strain the syrup into a clean container, discarding the solids. You can store the Hypocras syrup in the refrigerator for later use.

4. To make the Renaissance Elixir cocktail, combine the red wine, brandy, Hypocras syrup, fresh orange juice, and a dash of aromatic bitters in a mixing glass with ice.

5. Stir the ingredients until well chilled and properly diluted (usually about 30 seconds).

6. Strain the cocktail into a chilled coupe or cocktail glass.

7. Garnish with a twist of orange peel, expressing the oils over the drink by giving it a gentle twist to release its aroma.

Plums Roasted in Honey with a Medieval Flavor Profile

One true and intriguing medieval story involving plums is the tale of "The Miracle of the Five Gold Coins." This story is set in the 12th century and revolves around Saint Guillaume de Saint Pathus, also known as Saint William of Rochester.

According to legend, Saint William was a young boy who lived in England and served as a page in the household of a nobleman. One day, he was unjustly accused of theft and sentenced to death by hanging. Saint William prayed fervently for salvation, and, miraculously, plums rained down from the sky, cushioning his fall and saving his life.

The miraculous plum rainfall was seen as a divine intervention, and Saint William was spared from execution. His reputation as a holy figure grew, and he later became a canon regular and then a Prior. The story of the plum miracle became associated with him and was passed down through generations.

Saint William of Rochester is recognized as the patron saint of adopted children and is often depicted in religious art with plums falling around him. This medieval tale serves as a reminder of the enduring power of stories and legends that were woven into the fabric of medieval culture, often blending elements of faith, folklore, and nature.

Ingredients

- 6-8 ripe plums, halved and pitted
- 1/4 cup honey
- 1/4 cup red wine
- 1/4 tsp ground cinnamon
- 1/4 tsp ground ginger
- 1/4 tsp ground cloves
- 1/4 tsp ground nutmeg
- 1/4 tsp salt

Instructions

1. Preheat the oven to 375°F (190°C).
2. Arrange the plum halves, cut side up, in a baking dish.
3. In a small bowl, whisk together the honey, red wine, cinnamon, ginger, cloves, nutmeg, and salt.
4. Pour the honey mixture over the plums, making sure each half is coated.
5. Roast the plums for 20-25 minutes, or until they are tender and caramelized.
6. Serve warm with a dollop of whipped cream or vanilla ice cream, if desired.

Medieval-style Honeyed Wine-Stewed Cherries with Rose Water and Sweet Bread

One fascinating true story about rose water revolves around its use in the ancient city of Shiraz, which is now in modernday Iran. Shiraz is renowned for its long history of rose water production, dating back over a thousand years.

In the 9th century, during the Islamic Golden Age, Persian scientists and scholars were at the forefront of various fields, including chemistry and distillation. AlKindi, an Arab polymath, wrote extensively on the distillation of rose water, which was a significant advancement in the history of perfume and flavor extraction.

Rose water production in Shiraz became a highly specialized industry, with skilled distillers using an intricate process to extract the essence of roses. The process involved steam distillation, where the petals of specially cultivated Damask roses were heated, and the steam was condensed to yield the fragrant rose water.

The resulting rose water was not only valued for its exquisite scent but also for its culinary and medicinal properties. It found its way into the kitchens of Persia, where it was used to enhance the flavors of various dishes, including rice, pastries, and desserts. In addition, rose water was used in traditional Persian medicine for its supposed healing and soothing properties.

Over time, the fame of Shirazi rose water spread beyond the region, and it became a sought after commodity in trade.

Ingredients

- 1 1/2 lb. whole cherries
- 1/4 cup honey
- 1/4 cup sweet red wine
- 1/2 tsp. cinnamon
- 1/4 tsp. ginger
- Dash of rose water

Instructions
1. Remove the stems and pit the cherries.
2. In a saucepan, combine cherries, honey, sweet red wine, cinnamon, ginger, and rose water
3. Stew the mixture over medium heat for about 10 minutes, or until the cherries are soft and the flavors meld together.

Now, to the bread...

Medieval-style Sweet Bread (Buccellato) with Enriched Dough

Buccellato is a traditional Italian pastry, specifically associated with the region of Tuscany. It is a sweet, ring-shaped bread or cake that is often enjoyed during special occasions and holidays, particularly Christmas and Easter. Buccellato is traditionally associated with important holidays like Christmas and Easter in Tuscany. It's often baked in homes and bakeries during these festive seasons and is sometimes given as a gift to friends and family. You can make this recipe for whatever occasion needs to be elevated to a festive one.

To enrich the bread dough in the medieval style sweet bread recipe, you can add ingredients like sugar, raisins, and aniseed to the dough. Additionally, you can incorporate fats such as milk, butter, and/or eggs to make the dough richer and softer.

Ingredients

- 3 cups bread dough
- 1/4 cup sugar
- 1/2 cup raisins
- 1 tsp. aniseed
- 1/4 cup milk
- 1/4 cup softened butter
- 1 egg, beaten
- 1/4 cup milk or water (for egg wash)

Instructions

1. Prepare the bread dough according to your preferred recipe.
2. Mix in sugar, raisins, and aniseed to the dough.
3. Add milk, softened butter, and the beaten egg to the dough, and mix until well combined.
4. Shape the dough into a round loaf and place it on a greased baking sheet.
5. Cut the dough all the way around to help it rise better, and let it rest for at least an hour.
6. Preheat the oven to 375°F (190°C).
7. In a small bowl, beat the egg with milk or water to create an egg wash.
8. Brush the entire surface of the dough with the egg wash.
9. Let the dough rise again until doubled in size, then brush it with the egg wash once more.
10. Bake the bread for 35 minutes, or until golden brown and cooked through.

Remember to serve the enriched sweet bread with the honey-stewed cherries as mentioned in the previous recipe.

Pork in Grapes

The combination of pork and grapes has historical roots in Mediterranean and European cuisines. Grapes have long been cultivated in these regions, and pork was a staple meat source. The sweet and sour profile of the grapes provided a perfect counterpoint to the richness of the pork. In medieval and Renaissance European cookbooks, you can find recipes that feature pork with grapes, reflecting the culinary preferences of those times.

There are many regional variations of pork with grapes around the world. For example, in Italian cuisine, "Maiale al Latte" is a dish where pork is braised in milk and served with grapes.

Ingredients

- 4 pork chops
- 25g unsalted butter
- 1 tbsp nut oil
- 1 large onion, finely chopped
- 150ml single cream
- 250g seedless grapes (green or red)
- 200ml chicken stock
- Salt and freshly ground pepper

Instructions

1. Melt the butter and heat the nut oil in a pan.
2. Brown the pork chops on both sides and set them aside.
3. In the same pan, cook the chopped onion until it's soft and golden.
4. Add the chicken stock to the pan and bring it to a boil.
5. Return the pork chops to the pan, cover, and simmer for about 30 minutes or until the pork is cooked through.
6. Stir in the single cream and grapes, and cook for another 5 minutes.
7. Season with salt and freshly ground pepper to taste.

Serve Pork in Grapes with your choice of side dishes, such as rice, potatoes, or vegetables. Enjoy these delicious medieval-inspired main dishes!

Pork in Grapes : *Maiale al Latte* Version

This simplified Middle Ages-inspired Maiale al Latte recipe captures the essence of the dish, combining the sweetness of grapes and the richness of milk-cooked pork.

Maiale al Latte is believed to have originated in northern Italy, particularly in the regions of Lombardy and Emilia-Romagna. It's a rustic and hearty dish that reflects the culinary traditions of these regions. While its precise origin is challenging to pinpoint, it likely dates back many centuries.

Here's a simplified version of a Maiale al Latte recipe as it might have been prepared in the Middle Ages:

Ingredients:
- 2 pounds pork chops or pork tenderloin
- 2 cups milk
- 1 cup red or white grapes, halved and seeded
- 1 onion, chopped
- 2 cloves garlic, minced
- 2 tablespoons olive oil
- Salt and pepper, to taste
- Fresh rosemary or thyme, for seasoning

Instructions:
1. Heat olive oil in a large skillet or pan over medium-high heat.
2. Season the pork chops or tenderloin with salt and pepper. Brown them in the hot oil until they are golden on both sides. Remove the pork from the pan and set it aside.
3. In the same pan, add chopped onions and minced garlic. Sauté until the onions become translucent.
4. Return the pork to the pan, and add the milk. Bring the mixture to a simmer.
5. Lower the heat to medium-low, cover the pan, and let it cook gently for about 1 hour, turning the pork occasionally, until the meat is tender and cooked through. If the milk begins to curdle, it's okay; this is a characteristic of the dish.
6. Add the halved grapes to the pan and cook for an additional 10-15 minutes until the grapes soften and release their juices.
7. Adjust the seasoning with salt and pepper if needed. Garnish with fresh rosemary or thyme.
8. Serve the Maiale al Latte hot, with the grape and milk sauce spooned over the pork.

Pork in Grapes : Herbed Garum Pork Version

One well-known brand that produces a modern version of garum is "Colatura di Alici," which is often referred to as "Italian fish sauce." Colatura di Alici is produced in the Campania region of Italy, specifically in the town of Cetara on the Amalfi Coast. While it's not the same as the ancient Roman garum, it is inspired by historical fish sauces and has a similar umami-rich, salty, and briny flavor.

You can find Colatura di Alici in specialty food stores, gourmet markets, and online retailers that offer Italian or Mediterranean products. This condiment is typically used sparingly to season dishes and enhance their flavor.

Ingredients:

- 800g pork loin
- Summer Savory, pinch
- Thyme, pinch, fresh
- Dandelion Greens, 1/16th cup
- Spices (long pepper, bay laurel berries)
- Raisin wine
- Red wine
- Garum (ancient Roman fish sauce)
- Olive oil
- 1 cup seedless grapes (green or red)

Instructions
1. Pour olive oil and a bit of garum into a pan.
2. Cut the pork loin into pieces and cook it in the pan.
3. In a mortar, grind the spices (long pepper, bay laurel berries, thyme) with Savory . Tear and shred the Dandelion Greens.
4. Add the ground spices, raisin wine, and red wine to the pan with the pork.
5. Add the grapes to the pan.
6. Cook the pork and grapes in the sauce until the pork is tender and well-cooked.

Serve this delicious medieval-inspired main dish with your choice of side dishes, such as rice, potatoes, or vegetables. Enjoy the Drunken Pork with Grapes!

Simplified Homemade Garum

Please note that this homemade version is a simplified interpretation of garum, as true garum was a more complex and time-consuming process involving specific fish species and long fermentation periods. Nevertheless, this recipe can yield a flavorful and savory liquid condiment that can be used sparingly in various dishes to add depth of flavor. Adjust the fermentation time to your taste preference, with longer fermentation resulting in a stronger and more robust flavor.

Ingredients:

- 1 cup of small, salted fish (anchovies, sardines, or similar)
- 1 cup of water
- 1 tablespoon of sea salt
- 1 clove of garlic (optional)
- Fresh herbs (such as rosemary or thyme, optional)

Instructions:

1. Begin by thoroughly cleaning the small fish. Remove their heads, tails, and guts. Rinse them under cold water to remove excess salt.
2. Place the cleaned fish in a clean glass container, such as a glass jar or ceramic vessel.
3. In a separate container, dissolve the sea salt in water to create a brine solution.
4. Pour the brine solution over the fish in the container. Make sure the fish are fully submerged in the brine.
5. If desired, add a clove of garlic and a few sprigs of fresh herbs to the mixture. This can add additional flavor to your homemade garum.
6. Cover the container with a clean cloth or paper towel secured with a rubber band or string. This allows air to circulate while preventing dust and debris from entering.
7. Place the container in a warm, dark location for several weeks to several months, depending on the desired fermentation intensity. Check on it periodically.
8. During the fermentation process, the fish will break down, and the liquid will become rich in umami flavor. It will develop a strong aroma, somewhat reminiscent of soy sauce.
9. Once the desired flavor is achieved, strain the liquid through a fine mesh strainer to remove any solids. The resulting liquid is your homemade garum or garum-inspired sauce.
10. Store the garum in a sealed bottle or container in the refrigerator.

Spiced Fig and Honey Compote and Stuffed Figs with Medieval Spices

Spiced Fig and Honey Compote

Ingredients
- 1 lb fresh figs, quartered
- 1/4 cup honey
- 1/4 cup water
- 1/2 tsp cinnamon
- 1/4 tsp ginger
- 1/4 tsp cloves
- 1/4 tsp cardamom
- Pinch of saffron (optional)

Instructions
1. In a saucepan, combine figs, honey, water, cinnamon, ginger, cloves, cardamom, and saffron (if using).
2. Cook the mixture over medium-low heat, stirring occasionally, for about 20 minutes, or until the figs are soft and the sauce has thickened.
3. Allow the compote to cool slightly before serving. This compote can be served with cheese, bread, or as a topping for desserts.

Stuffed Figs with Medieval Spices

Ingredients
- 12 fresh figs
- 1/2 cup ricotta cheese
- 1/4 cup honey
- 1/4 tsp cinnamon
- 1/4 tsp ginger
- 1/4 tsp cloves
- 1/4 tsp cardamom
- 1/4 cup chopped walnuts or almonds

Instructions
1. Preheat the oven to 350°F (175°C).
2. Cut a small slit in the top of each fig, creating an opening for the stuffing.
3. In a bowl, mix together ricotta cheese, honey, cinnamon, ginger, cloves, cardamom, and chopped nuts.
4. Stuff each fig with the ricotta mixture, using a small spoon or piping bag.
5. Place the stuffed figs on a baking sheet lined with parchment paper.
6. Bake for 15-20 minutes, or until the figs are tender and the filling is slightly golden.
7. Allow the figs to cool slightly before serving. Enjoy!

Olive and Fig Salad with Medieval Spices

The combination of olives and figs is a classic pairing in Mediterranean cuisine, and it has deep historical roots. The practice of combining olives and figs dates back to ancient times when both of these ingredients were essential components of the Mediterranean diet. Both olives and figs were widely cultivated and consumed in various Mediterranean regions. Olives and figs were well-suited to the Mediterranean climate and became staple crops. Olive trees thrived in the rocky, sun-soaked terrains, while fig trees flourished in the warm and dry conditions.

In some cultures, olives and figs held symbolic significance. Olives were often associated with peace and prosperity, while figs symbolized fertility and abundance. This symbolism may have influenced their use together in celebratory meals.

Ingredients

- 1 cup pitted olives
- 1 cup fresh figs, quartered
- 1/4 cup chopped walnuts
- 1/4 cup crumbled feta cheese
- 2 tbsp olive oil
- 1 tbsp red wine vinegar
- 1/2 tsp cinnamon
- 1/4 tsp ginger
- 1/4 tsp cloves
- Salt and pepper to taste

Instructions
1. In a large bowl, combine the olives, figs, chopped walnuts, and crumbled feta cheese.
2. In a small bowl, whisk together the olive oil, red wine vinegar, cinnamon, ginger, cloves, salt, and pepper.
3. Pour the dressing over the olive and fig mixture and toss to coat.
4. Serve the salad chilled or at room temperature.

This salad is a unique and flavorful way to incorporate olives and figs into a medieval-themed meal. Enjoy the Olive and Fig Salad with Medieval Spices!

Medieval Spiced Sausage and Quince Paste Sauce with a Side of Mashed Sweet Potatoes

Medieval Spiced Sausage and Quince Paste Sauce

Ingredients

- 4 spiced sausages
- 1/2 cup quince paste
- 1/4 cup red wine
- 1/4 cup chicken broth
- 1/2 tsp cinnamon
- 1/4 tsp ginger
- 1/4 tsp cloves
- Salt and pepper to taste

Instructions

1. Preheat the oven to 375°F (190°C).
2. Place the spiced sausages on a baking sheet and bake for 20-25 minutes, or until cooked through.
3. In a saucepan, combine the quince paste, red wine, chicken broth, cinnamon, ginger, cloves, salt, and pepper.
4. Cook the sauce over medium heat, stirring occasionally, for about 10 minutes, or until the quince paste has melted and the sauce has thickened.
5. Serve the spiced sausages with the quince paste sauce drizzled on top.

Mashed Sweet Potatoes

Ingredients

- 2 large sweet potatoes, peeled and cubed
- 1/4 cup milk
- 2 tbsp butter
- Salt and pepper to taste

Instructions:

1. Boil the sweet potatoes in a pot of salted water for 15-20 minutes, or until tender.
2. Drain the sweet potatoes and return them to the pot.
3. Add the milk and butter to the pot and mash the sweet potatoes until smooth.
4. Season with salt and pepper to taste.

Serve the Medieval Spiced Sausage and Quince Paste Sauce with a side of Mashed Sweet Potatoes for a delicious and hearty medieval-themed meal. Enjoy!

Medieval Spiced Sausage

The origin of medieval spiced sausage can be traced back to ancient times, as sausages were a convenient and portable way to preserve meat.. The earliest appearance of a type of blood sausage was mentioned around 800 BC in Book 18 of Homer's Odyssey.

Sausages were popular with both the ancient Greeks and the Romans, and most likely with the various tribes occupying the larger part of Europe. In the Roman Empire, sausages were made with a variety of meats and spices, including Lucanian sausages, which were cold-smoked sausages that were grilled and served with a sweet and spicy fish sauce

In the Middle Ages, sausages continued to be a popular food, and different regions developed their own unique recipes and flavors. Medieval spiced sausage likely evolved from these regional variations, with spices such as cinnamon, ginger, cloves, and nutmeg being added to the meat mixture for flavor.

Ingredients

- 1 lb ground pork
- 1/2 tsp cinnamon
- 1/4 tsp ginger
- 1/4 tsp cloves
- 1/4 tsp nutmeg
- 1/4 tsp black pepper
- 1/4 tsp salt
- 1 tbsp red wine vinegar
- 1 tbsp honey

Instructions
1. In a large bowl, mix together the ground pork, cinnamon, ginger, cloves, nutmeg, black pepper, and salt.
2. Add the red wine vinegar and honey to the bowl and mix until well combined.
3. Cover the bowl with plastic wrap and refrigerate for at least 1 hour, or overnight.
4. Form the sausage mixture into patties or links.
5. Heat a skillet over medium-high heat and cook the sausage patties or links until browned and cooked through, about 45 minutes per side.

Serve the Medieval Spiced Sausage with a side of Quince Paste Sauce and Mashed Sweet Potatoes for a delicious and hearty medieval-themed meal. Enjoy!

Medieval-Flavoured Melon and Anchovy Appetizer

In Medieval Europe, monastic gardens played a significant role in the cultivation of fruits and vegetables, including melons. Monasteries often had the resources and knowledge to grow a variety of crops, and melons were occasionally cultivated in their gardens.

Melons, when available, were used in both sweet and savory medieval recipes. They were used to make dishes like fruit tarts, preserves, and sometimes even soups.

Anchovies played a notable role in medieval European cuisine, particularly in coastal regions and areas with access to the sea. Anchovies were sometimes used as a general tonic or restorative food. They were believed to provide strength and vitality, making them a popular choice for convalescents and those recovering from illness.

In traditional medicine, anchovies were used to alleviate inflammation and joint pain. The belief was that their salty and savory qualities could help reduce swelling and discomfort. And, like many foods with strong or unusual flavors, anchovies were occasionally considered aphrodisiacs. They were believed to have properties that could increase desire and sexual potency.

Ingredients

- 1/2 melon, cut into bite-sized pieces
- 1 can of anchovies, drained and chopped
- 1/4 cup chopped almonds
- 1/4 cup chopped fresh parsley
- 1/4 tsp ground cinnamon
- 1/4 tsp ground ginger
- 1/4 tsp ground cloves
- 1/4 tsp black pepper
- 1 tbsp honey
- 1 tbsp red wine vinegar
- 1 tbsp olive oil
- Pinch of salt

Instructions:
1. In a small bowl, whisk together the chopped anchovies, chopped almonds, chopped parsley, ground cinnamon, ground ginger, ground cloves, black pepper, honey, red wine vinegar, olive oil, and salt.
2. In a large bowl, add the cubed melon.
3. Pour the dressing over the melon and toss to coat.
4. Chill the salad in the refrigerator for at least 30 minutes before serving.

This Medieval Flavoured Melon and Anchovy Appetizer is a unique and flavourful dish that is perfect for a medieval-themed party or gathering. Enjoy!

Acorn Squash Ice Cream with Medieval Spiced Chocolate Syrup

Ice cream, as we know it today, did not exist in the medieval ages. There was Sorbets and Sherbet. There was flavoured ice and , in some European courts, it was customary to serve dishes that were cooled with ice or snow. Special containers, often made of metal, were used to keep the food cold during feasts and banquets. These might include fruit salads or sweetened creambased dishes. Let's go anachronistic. Let's go odd. Acorn Squash Ice Cream could be the hit of your Medieval Garden Harvest Party!

Ingredients

- 1 acorn squash
- 2 tablespoons butter
- 1 tablespoon water, or as needed
- 4 egg yolks
- 1/2 cup light brown sugar
- 2 cups heavy whipping cream
- 1 teaspoon vanilla extract
- Pinch of salt

Instructions
1. Preheat the oven to 375°F (190°C).
2. Cut the acorn squash in half and remove the seeds.
3. Place the squash halves on a baking sheet and brush with melted butter and water.
4. Bake the squash for 45-50 minutes, or until soft and tender.
5. Allow the squash to cool, then scoop out the flesh and discard the skin.
6. In a large bowl, whisk together the egg yolks and brown sugar until light and fluffy.
7. In a saucepan, heat the heavy cream over medium heat until it begins to steam.
8. Slowly pour the hot cream into the egg mixture, whisking constantly.
9. Pour the mixture back into the saucepan and cook over low heat, stirring constantly, until it thickens and coats the back of a spoon.
10. Remove the mixture from the heat and stir in the squash puree, vanilla extract, and salt.
11. Allow the mixture to cool, then chill it in the refrigerator for at least 2 hours.
12. Pour the chilled mixture into an ice cream maker and churn according to the manufacturer's instructions.
13. Transfer the ice cream to a container and freeze for at least 2 hours before serving.

Medieval Spiced Chocolate Syrup

Chocolate in its solid, edible form did not become popular in Europe until the late 16th and early 17th centuries, well after the medieval period. However, chocolate as a beverage made from cacao beans was known to Europeans during the later medieval and early Renaissance periods. So, this is a bit on the anachronistic side. Then again, it is all an experiment, so let's try this one. If the Acorn Squash Ice Cream send you for a loop, this topping will work on vanilla bean ice cream just as well.

Ingredients

- 1/2 cup cocoa powder
- 1/2 cup sugar
- 1/2 cup water
- 1/4 tsp cinnamon
- 1/4 tsp ginger
- 1/4 tsp cloves
- Pinch of salt

Instructions
1. In a saucepan, whisk together the cocoa powder, sugar, water, cinnamon, ginger, cloves, and salt.
2. Cook the mixture over medium heat, stirring constantly, until it thickens and becomes syrupy.
3. Remove the mixture from the heat and allow it to cool.

To serve, scoop the Acorn Squash Ice Cream into bowls and drizzle with the Medieval Spiced Chocolate Syrup. Enjoy this unique and delicious dessert that combines the flavours of medieval spices with the sweetness of acorn squash ice cream.

Garliced Orache Soup with Cream Dollop and Saffron

Orache, also known as French Spinach, is a leafy vegetable that was common in medieval gardens. It is a species of plant in the amaranth family and is used as a leaf vegetable. Orache is also known as garden orache, red orache, mountain spinach, French spinach, or arrach. It is a medium to tall plant with ridged stems and arrow-shaped or diamond-shaped leaves. Orache is a salt-loving plant and can be found in coastal regions and along salt playas in landlocked regions. It is a warm-weather alternative to spinach and is still grown as a leafy vegetable today. Orache is edible and can be used in a variety of dishes, such as salads, soups, and stews.

Ingredients

- 6-7 bunches of orache (about 150g once trimmed of stems)
- 1 onion, chopped
- 2 garlic cloves, minced
- 1 tbsp olive oil
- 4 cups vegetable broth
- 1/2 cup heavy cream
- 1/4 tsp saffron threads
- Salt and pepper to taste

Instructions
1. Wash the orache leaves and remove the stems.
2. In a large pot, heat the olive oil over medium heat.
3. Add the chopped onion and minced garlic and sauté until the onion is translucent.
4. Add the orache leaves to the pot and stir to combine.
5. Pour in the vegetable broth and bring the mixture to a boil.
6. Reduce the heat to low and simmer for 20-25 minutes, or until the orache is tender.
7. Remove the pot from the heat and let it cool slightly.
8. Using an immersion blender, puree the soup until smooth.
9. Return the soup to the pot and stir in the heavy cream and saffron threads.
10. Season with salt and pepper to taste.
11. Serve the soup hot, garnished with a dollop of whipped cream and a sprinkle of saffron threads.

Orache

Orache is a hardy plant that can tolerate a range of growing conditions, including poor soil and drought. It is a great addition to any garden and can be used in a variety of dishes, such as salads, soups, and stews.

Orache is a leafy vegetable that is also known by several other names. Here are some other popular names for orache:

- Garden orache
- Red orache
- Mountain spinach
- French spinach
- Arrach
- Saltbush
- Red goosefoot
- Quinoa
- Goosefoot
- Herbaceous plant

These names are commonly used to refer to orache in different regions and contexts. Orache is a species of plant in the amaranth family and is used as a leaf vegetable. It was common before spinach and is still grown as a warm-weather alternative to that crop.

Medieval-inspired Orache (French Spinach) with Pork Belly and Quail Eggs

Orache can sometimes be found in specialty or organic markets, but it's less common than other leafy greens like spinach and Swiss chard.

Ingredients

- 1 pound orache or French spinach (you can substitute with spinach or Swiss chard)
- 1/2 pound pork belly, diced
- 1 small onion, finely chopped
- 2 cloves garlic, minced
- 1/2 teaspoon ground black pepper
- Salt to taste
- 1/2 cup chicken or vegetable broth
- Olive oil for cooking
- 4 quail eggs (unusual ingredient)

Instructions

1. Heat a large skillet or pan over medium heat. Add a little olive oil, then add the diced pork belly. Cook until it becomes crispy and golden brown. Remove the pork belly from the pan and set it aside.
2. In the same pan, add the chopped onion and minced garlic. Sauté until the onion is translucent and fragrant.
3. Add the orache or French spinach to the pan. If the leaves are large, you can chop them into smaller pieces. Cook the orache until it wilts and becomes tender, which should only take a few minutes.
4. Season the orache with black pepper and a pinch of salt.
5. Return the crispy pork belly to the pan and stir to combine.
6. Pour in the chicken or vegetable broth and simmer for a few minutes until everything is well heated and the flavors have melded together.
7. While the dish is simmering, in a separate pan, cook the quail eggs to your desired level of doneness (poached, fried, or boiled).
8. To serve, place the quail eggs on top of the orache and pork belly mixture. Adjust the seasoning if necessary and enjoy your unique medieval-inspired dish.

Medieval-Inspired Orache (French Spinach) with Lemon and Thyme, and Candied Pecans

Here is a unique and experimental recipe that combines candied pecans with orache (French spinach) for a sweet and savory dish. This recipe is a creative twist that allows you to enjoy the flavors of candied pecans alongside the mild, slightly salty taste of orache.

Ingredients

- 1 pound orache or French spinach (or spinach)
- Zest of 1 lemon
- Juice of 1 lemon
- 23 sprigs of fresh thyme, leaves removed
- 2 tablespoons butter
- Salt and black pepper to taste

Instructions
1. In a large pot or skillet, melt the butter over medium heat.
2. Add the orache (or French spinach) to the pot and sauté until it wilts and becomes tender. This should only take a few minutes.
3. Add the lemon zest, lemon juice, and fresh thyme leaves to the orache. Stir to combine and allow the flavors to meld for a couple of minutes.
4. Season with salt and black pepper to taste.
5. Just before serving, sprinkle the candied pecans over the orache, lemon, and thyme dish for a delightful sweet crunch.
6. Serve your medieval-inspired orache with lemon, thyme, and candied pecans as a unique side dish, garnished with a few extra thyme leaves if desired.

Orache Terrine

Terrines in the Middle Ages often featured a combination of ingredients like seafood, eggs, and leafy greens, resulting in flavorful and visually appealing dishes. Seafood, such as fish and shellfish, was a prized component of medieval cuisine, often considered a delicacy. Eggs were also a common ingredient, used for their binding and thickening properties. Leafy greens, including spinach and various wild greens, were utilized to provide color, texture, and a hint of freshness to the dish.

The preparation of a terrine typically involved layering ingredients in a loaf-shaped mold, often made of earthenware, and then baking it. This cooking method helped meld the flavors and set the dish. Spices and seasonings were used to enhance the taste, with herbs like thyme, parsley, and sage being popular choices.

In the Middle Ages, terrines were commonly served at banquets and feasts, where they were often elaborate and showcased the culinary skills of the cooks. They could contain various ingredients, depending on availability and the host's wealth. Seafood, eggs, and leafy greens would have been part of the broader medieval culinary repertoire, contributing to the richness and complexity of terrine recipes. These dishes were a testament to the culinary sophistication of the time, and their legacy continues to influence modern charcuterie and pâté traditions.

French Spinach and Shrimp Terrine with Medieval Flavors

Creating a French spinach and shrimp terrine with a medieval flavor profile can be a unique and interesting culinary endeavor. The following is a creative recipe that combines the modern concept of a terrine with ingredients and flavors inspired by the medieval period. This terrine features orache (French spinach) and shrimp as the main components and incorporates medieval-inspired seasonings and spices for a historical twist.

Since this one is a bit on the challenging side, the format that follows has been expanded.

Ingredients

* For the Terrine
- 1 pound orache (French spinach), blanched and chopped
- 1 pound shrimp, peeled and de-veined
- 1 cup heavy cream
- 4 large eggs
- 1/2 cup grated Parmesan cheese
- 1/4 cup almond flour (to mimic medieval almond milk)
- 1/4 teaspoon ground nutmeg
- 1/4 teaspoon ground cloves
- Salt and black pepper to taste
- Butter for greasing the terrine mold

* For the Garnish
- Whole orache leaves or edible flowers (medieval garnishes)

Instructions

Prepare the Terrine

1. Preheat your oven to 350°F (175°C).

2. In a food processor, combine the blanched and chopped orache (French spinach), shrimp, and almond flour. Process until you have a smooth, uniform mixture.

3. In a separate bowl, whisk together the eggs and heavy cream.

4. Add the egg and cream mixture to the orache and shrimp mixture in the food processor. Blend until well combined.

5. Season the mixture with grated Parmesan cheese, ground nutmeg, ground cloves, salt, and black pepper. Pulse to incorporate the seasonings.

6. Grease a terrine mold with butter. The terrine mold should be suitable for baking, and it should have a lid.

7. Pour the orache and shrimp mixture into the terrine mold.

8. Cover the terrine mold with its lid or with aluminum foil.

Bake the Terrine

1. Place the terrine mold in a larger baking dish or roasting pan.

2. Add hot water to the larger dish until it reaches about halfway up the sides of the terrine mold. This creates a water bath (bainmarie) to ensure even and gentle cooking.

3. Bake in the preheated oven for about 60-75 minutes, or until the terrine is set and a knife inserted into the center comes out clean.

Chill and Serve

1. Once the terrine is done, remove it from the oven and allow it to cool to room temperature.

2. Refrigerate the terrine for several hours or overnight to firm up.

3. To serve, carefully un-mold the terrine onto a platter or serving dish.

4. Garnish the terrine with whole orache leaves or edible flowers to add a medieval touch.

This French spinach and shrimp terrine combines the modern concept of a terrine with medieval-inspired flavors to create a unique and visually appealing dish. Enjoy this fusion of flavors and textures.

VI

Medicinal Uses of Plants in Medieval Gardens

The gardens of medieval Europe were not just sources of culinary delights and ornamental beauty; they also served as apothecaries for the body and soul. In these carefully tended plots, a vast array of medicinal plants flourished, each with its own unique power to heal, soothe, and strengthen.

The Herbal Apothecary

The herbal apothecary was integral to medieval European society from the 11th to the 15th centuries. During this time, monastic orders and medical schools played a crucial role in the cultivation of herbs, development of herbal remedies, and dissemination of herbal knowledge.

The herbal apothecary of the Middle Ages was a vital institution, often nestled within monastery walls or town squares. Here, skilled apothecaries and herbalists diligently cultivated, prepared, and dispensed a wide array of botanical remedies. They harnessed the knowledge of ancient texts, blending the mystical with the practical. Aromatic herbs like lavender and sage were dried and stored alongside potent elixirs brewed from yarrow and chamomile. These apothecaries were trusted healers, offering salves, tinctures, and potions to treat ailments ranging from fevers to wounds. Their legacy lives on, shaping modern herbal medicine and reminding us of the enduring power of nature's pharmacy.

Medicinal Uses of Plants in Medieval Gardens

Medieval gardens were not only a source of food and beauty but also a source of medicine. The plants grown in medieval gardens were used for a variety of medicinal purposes, from treating common ailments to more serious illnesses. In this article, we will explore 15 plants that were commonly grown in medieval gardens, where they were grown and used, the history of each plant, suitable soil and conditions to grow each plant, companion planting, medicinal uses in the Middle Ages, contemporary research on their properties, and folklore about each.

1. Chamomile (*Matricaria chamomilla*)
Chamomile was a popular medicinal herb in medieval gardens. It was used to treat a variety of ailments, including digestive problems, anxiety, and insomnia. Chamomile was also used as a natural remedy for skin conditions such as eczema and psoriasis. Chamomile prefers well-draining soil and full sun. It can be grown alongside other herbs such as lavender and rosemary.

2. Sage (*Salvia officinalis*)
Sage was another popular medicinal herb in medieval gardens. It was used to treat sore throats, coughs, and digestive problems. Sage was also used as a natural remedy for hot flashes and other menopausal symptoms. Sage prefers well-draining soil and full sun. It can be grown alongside other herbs such as thyme and oregano.

3. Lavender (*Lavandula angustifolia*)
Lavender was a popular medicinal herb in medieval gardens. It was used to treat headaches, anxiety, and insomnia. Lavender was also used as a natural remedy for skin conditions such as acne and eczema. Lavender prefers well-draining soil and full sun. It can be grown alongside other herbs such as rosemary and thyme.

4. Rosemary (*Rosmarinus officinalis*)
Rosemary was another popular medicinal herb in medieval gardens. It was used to treat headaches, digestive problems, and memory loss. Rosemary was also used as a natural remedy for hair loss and dandruff. Rosemary prefers well-draining soil and full sun. It can be grown alongside other herbs such as thyme and oregano.

5. Thyme (*Thymus vulgaris*)
Thyme was a popular medicinal herb in medieval gardens. It was used to treat respiratory infections, digestive problems, and skin conditions. Thyme was also used as a natural remedy for bad breath and toothaches. Thyme prefers well-draining soil and full sun. It can be grown alongside other herbs such as rosemary and oregano.

6. Calendula (*Calendula officinalis*)
Calendula was a popular medicinal herb in medieval gardens. It was used to treat skin conditions such as cuts, burns, and rashes. Calendula was also used

as a natural remedy for digestive problems and menstrual cramps. Calendula prefers well-draining soil and full sun. It can be grown alongside other herbs such as chamomile and lavender.

7. Yarrow (*Achillea millefolium*)
Yarrow was another popular medicinal herb in medieval gardens. It was used to treat wounds, fever, and digestive problems. Yarrow was also used as a natural remedy for menstrual cramps and other gynecological issues. Yarrow prefers well-draining soil and full sun. It can be grown alongside other herbs such as chamomile and lavender.

8. Comfrey (*Symphytum officinale*)
Comfrey was a popular medicinal herb in medieval gardens. It was used to treat wounds, bruises, and broken bones. Comfrey was also used as a natural remedy for respiratory infections and digestive problems. Comfrey prefers moist soil and partial shade. It can be grown alongside other herbs such as mint and lemon balm.

9. Lemon Balm (*Melissa officinalis*)
Lemon balm was another popular medicinal herb in medieval gardens. It was used to treat anxiety, insomnia, and digestive problems. Lemon balm was also used as a natural remedy for cold sores and other viral infections. Lemon balm prefers well-draining soil and partial shade. It can be grown alongside other herbs such as mint and comfrey.

10. Mint (*Mentha spp.*)
Mint was a popular medicinal herb in medieval gardens. It was used to treat digestive problems, headaches, and respiratory infections. Mint was also used as a natural remedy for bad breath and toothaches. Mint prefers moist soil and partial shade. It can be grown alongside other herbs such as lemon balm and comfrey.

11. Fennel (*Foeniculum vulgare*)
Fennel was another popular medicinal herb in medieval gardens. It was used to treat digestive problems, menstrual cramps, and respiratory infections. Fennel was also used as a natural remedy for colic in infants. Fennel prefers well-draining soil and full sun. It can be grown alongside other herbs such as chamomile and lavender.

12. Dandelion (*Taraxacum officinale*)
Dandelion was a popular medicinal herb in medieval gardens. It was used to treat digestive problems, liver problems, and skin conditions. Dandelion was also used as a natural remedy for high blood pressure and other cardiovascular issues. Dandelion prefers well-draining soil and full sun. It can be grown alongside other herbs such as chamomile and lavender.

Dandelion greens, leaves, and roots were commonly used in medieval European cuisine. The young leaves were often incorporated into salads or cooked as greens. The roots were sometimes roasted and used as a coffee substitute, similar to chicory. Dandelions were valued for their medicinal properties in medieval times. They were believed to have various health benefits, such as promoting digestion and acting as a diuretic. Dandelion root tea, made by steeping the dried roots in hot water, was often used for its supposed health benefits.

Dandelions were sometimes used in brewing, particularly in traditional ales. They were added to impart flavor and bitterness to the beer. And, Dandelion flowers and roots were used for dyeing textiles. The flowers could produce a yellow or greenish dye, while the roots could create a brownish or reddish color. There is an amazingly deep tradition with this plant that 20th C. households think is a weed. Could be time for the general public to rethink this one.

13. Elderberry (*Sambucus nigra*)
Elderberry was another popular medicinal herb in medieval gardens. It was used to treat respiratory infections, fever, and digestive problems. Elderberry was also used as a natural remedy for colds and flu. Elderberry prefers well-draining soil and full sun. It can be grown alongside other herbs such as chamomile and lavender.

14. St. John's Wort (*Hypericum perforatum*)
St. John's Wort was a popular medicinal herb in medieval gardens. It was used to treat depression, anxiety, and nerve pain. St. John's Wort was also used as a natural remedy for skin conditions such as burns and bruises. St. John's Wort prefers well-draining soil and full sun. It can be grown alongside other herbs such as chamomile and lavender.

15. Angelica (*Angelica archangelica*)
Angelica was another popular medicinal herb in medieval gardens. It was used to treat digestive problems, respiratory infections, and menstrual cramps. Angelica was also used as a natural remedy for anxiety and insomnia. Angelica prefers moist soil and partial shade. It can be grown alongside other herbs such as mint and lemon balm.

In conclusion, medieval gardens were not only a source of food and beauty but also a source of medicine. The plants grown in medieval gardens were used for a variety of medicinal purposes, from treating common ailments to more serious illnesses. The 15 plants listed above were commonly grown in medieval gardens and were used for a variety of medicinal purposes. They can still be grown today and used for their medicinal properties, as well as for their beauty and culinary uses.

Researching, I thought that there must be more, so here are 14 more plants commonly found in medieval gardens, along with their history, medicinal uses, and growing conditions:

1. . Borage (*Borago officinalis*)
Borage was a popular medicinal herb in medieval gardens. It was used to treat respiratory infections, digestive problems, and skin conditions. Borage prefers well-draining soil and full sun.

2. Chervil (*Anthriscus cerefolium*)
Chervil was a popular medicinal herb in medieval gardens. It was used to treat digestive problems, respiratory infections, and menstrual cramps. Chervil prefers well-draining soil and partial shade.

3. Costmary (*Tanacetum balsamita*)
Costmary was a popular medicinal herb in medieval gardens. It was used to treat digestive problems, respiratory infections, and menstrual cramps. Costmary prefers well-draining soil and full sun.

4. Dittany (*Origanum dictamnus*)
Dittany was a popular medicinal herb in medieval gardens. It was used to treat respiratory infections, digestive problems, and menstrual cramps. Dittany prefers well-draining soil and full sun.

5. Elecampane (*Inula helenium*)
Elecampane was a popular medicinal herb in medieval gardens. It was used to treat respiratory infections, digestive problems, and menstrual cramps. Elecampane prefers well-draining soil and full sun.

6. Hyssop (*Hyssopus officinalis*)
Hyssop was a popular medicinal herb in medieval gardens. It was used to treat respiratory infections, digestive problems, and menstrual cramps. Hyssop prefers well-draining soil and full sun.

7. Lemon Verbena (*Aloysia citrodora*)
Lemon verbena was a popular medicinal herb in medieval gardens. It was used to treat digestive problems, respiratory infections, and menstrual cramps. Lemon verbena prefers well-draining soil and full sun.

8. Lovage (*Levisticum officinale*)
Lovage was a popular medicinal herb in medieval gardens. It was used to treat digestive problems, respiratory infections, and menstrual cramps. Lovage prefers well-draining soil and full sun.

9. Marigold (*Calendula officinalis*)
Marigold was a popular medicinal herb in medieval gardens. It was used to treat skin conditions such as cuts, burns, and rashes. Marigold prefers well-draining soil and full sun.

10. Rue (*Ruta graveolens*)
Rue was a popular medicinal herb in medieval gardens. It was used to treat digestive problems, respiratory infections, and menstrual cramps. Rue prefers well-draining soil and full sun. Many cuisines have developed alternatives to rue that provide similar flavors without the bitterness or toxicity concerns. Herbs like thyme, oregano, and rosemary are more commonly used in contemporary cooking to achieve similar flavor profiles.

11. Sorrel (*Rumex acetosa*)
Sorrel was a popular medicinal herb in medieval gardens. It was used to treat

digestive problems, respiratory infections, and menstrual cramps. Sorrel prefers well-draining soil and full sun.

Sorrel was a common ingredient in medieval European cooking. Its tart flavor, reminiscent of lemon, made it a valuable addition to various dishes. Sorrel was used to add acidity and a refreshing taste to soups, sauces, stews, and salads. It was particularly popular in fish and poultry dishes.

Sorrel was also valued for its potential medicinal properties in medieval herbalism. It was believed to have diuretic and cooling effects, and it was used to treat ailments related to digestion and fevers.

Sorrel soups were a common preparation during medieval times. These soups often combined sorrel with other ingredients like broth, eggs, and sometimes cream.

12. Tansy (*Tanacetum vulgare*)

Tansy was a popular medicinal herb in medieval gardens. It was used to treat digestive problems, respiratory infections, and menstrual cramps. Tansy prefers well-draining soil and full sun.

Tansy had symbolic meanings in medieval Europe. It was sometimes associated with immortality and was used in floral wreaths and garlands for festive occasions. In addition to its culinary and insect-repelling uses, tansy was employed in various herbal remedies. It was believed to have the ability to expel worms, and tansy infusions were used for this purpose.

There are toxicity concerns when used illiberally. As with all herbs on any list, it is best to research and use appropriately.

13. Wormwood (*Artemisia absinthium*)

Wormwood was a popular medicinal herb in medieval gardens. It was used to treat digestive problems, respiratory infections, and menstrual cramps. Wormwood prefers well-draining soil and full sun.

14. Yarrow (*Achillea millefolium*)

Yarrow was a popular medicinal herb in medieval gardens. It was one of the most widely used medicinal herbs in medieval Europe. It was used to treat wounds, fever, and digestive problems. Yarrow was also used as a natural remedy for menstrual cramps and other gynecological issues. Yarrow prefers well-draining soil and full sun.

Yarrow had a place in medieval folklore and superstitions. It was believed to have protective qualities and was sometimes used in charms and amulets.

Time to revisit this traditional herb.

Tinctures and Balms

Tinctures and balms have been integral to herbal medicine throughout history.

Tinctures, made by macerating herbs in alcohol, vinegar, or glycerin, have ancient roots, with herbalists like Paracelsus advocating for their use in the 16th century. They deliver potent herbal properties and have long shelf lives, making them valuable tools in traditional healing practices.

Balms, on the other hand, find their origins in the herbal ointments of ancient civilizations like Egypt and Greece. These semi-solid mixtures, infused with herbs or essential oils, were prized for their topical application, offering relief for skin conditions, muscle aches, and more. Today, both tinctures and balms continue to bridge the gap between herbal tradition and modern wellness.

Rosemary Tincture

Improved cognition.
Anti-inflammatory effects.
Antioxidant protection.
Digestive aid.
Antimicrobial properties.
Pain relief.
Respiratory support.
Stress reduction.
Hair and scalp health.
Skin soothing.

Ingredients
- Fresh rosemary leaves
- High-proof alcohol (such as vodka or brandy)

Instructions
1. Chop fresh rosemary leaves to increase the surface area for the maceration and place them into a sterilized jar, filling it to 3/4 full.
2. Pour high-proof alcohol to the very top of the jar to cover the rosemary completely.
3. Seal the jar and let it sit for several weeks, shaking it daily to ensure the plant material is evenly distributed.
4. After several weeks, strain the mixture and store the herbal tincture in a dark glass bottle.

Lavender Balm

Relaxation and stress reduction.
Improved sleep quality.
Pain relief, including headaches.
Skin soothing and wound healing.
Anti-inflammatory properties.
Antioxidant effects.
Respiratory support.
Digestive aid.
Hair and scalp health.
Insect repellent.

Ingredients
- Dried lavender flowers
- Oil (such as olive oil or coconut oil)
- Beeswax

Instructions
1. Infuse dried lavender flowers in oil by placing them in a jar and covering them with oil. Let sit for several weeks, shaking occasionally.
2. Strain the oil and discard the lavender flowers.
3. Melt beeswax in a double boiler.
4. Add the infused oil to the melted beeswax and stir until well combined.
5. Pour the mixture into a container and let it cool and solidify.

Ginger Tincture

Digestive aid, alleviating nausea and indigestion.
Anti-inflammatory properties, reducing pain and inflammation.
Immune system support.
Motion sickness relief.
Pain relief for headaches and menstrual cramps.
Lowering blood sugar levels.
Antioxidant effects.
Improved circulation.
Respiratory support.
Arthritis pain relief.

Ingredients
- Fresh ginger root
- High-proof alcohol (such as vodka or brandy)

Instructions
1. Chop fresh ginger root to increase the surface area for the maceration and place it into a sterilized jar, filling it to 3/4 full.
2. Pour high-proof alcohol to the very top of the jar to cover the ginger completely.
3. Seal the jar and let it sit for several weeks, shaking it daily to ensure the plant material is evenly distributed.
4. After several weeks, strain the mixture and store the herbal tincture in a dark glass bottle.

Chamomile Balm

Relaxation and improved sleep.
Digestive aid, relieving indigestion and gas.
Anti-inflammatory effects for skin and internal issues.
Immune system support.
Menstrual pain relief.
Skin soothing and wound healing.
Respiratory support.
Stress reduction.
Allergy relief.
Hair and scalp health.

Ingredients:
- Dried chamomile flowers
- Oil (such as olive oil or coconut oil)
- Beeswax

Instructions:
1. Infuse dried chamomile flowers in oil by placing them in a jar and covering them with oil. Let sit for several weeks, shaking occasionally.
2. Strain the oil and discard the chamomile flowers.
3. Melt beeswax in a double boiler.
4. Add the infused oil to the melted beeswax and stir until well combined.
5. Pour the mixture into a container and let it cool and solidify.

Cinnamon Tincture

Blood sugar regulation.
Anti-inflammatory properties.
Antioxidant effects.
Improved heart health.
Lowering cholesterol levels.
Enhanced cognitive function.
Anti-microbial properties.
Digestive aid.
Pain relief.
Skin health support.

Ingredients:
- Cinnamon sticks
- High-proof alcohol (such as vodka or brandy)

Instructions:
1. Break cinnamon sticks into small pieces to increase the surface area for the maceration and place them into a sterilized jar, filling it to 3/4 full.
2. Pour high-proof alcohol to the very top of the jar to cover the cinnamon completely.
3. Seal the jar and let it sit for several weeks, shaking it daily to ensure the plant material is evenly distributed.
4. After several weeks, strain the mixture and store the herbal tincture in a dark glass bottle.

VII
Medlar & Crabapple

are two fruits that stands out as both intriguing and versatile, offering a glimpse into the culinary ingenuity of the time.

The medlar, with its enigmatic and captivating journey from a seemingly unpalatable, rock-hard fruit to a luscious, honeyed delicacy, is a unique and often overlooked jewel in the treasure chest of medieval cuisine. Revered for its ability to transform through the intriguing process of bletting, the medlar found a cherished place in medieval culinary traditions. Its complex flavors, reminiscent of spiced apples and dates, made it an essential ingredient for tarts, puddings, jellies, and preserves

The crabapple, with its tart and crisp flesh, offered a burst of flavor that complemented both sweet and savory dishes. Renowned for its resilience and versatility, the crabapple was not merely a staple but a culinary chameleon, finding its place in hearty stews, delicate preserves, and even in the production of tangy ales and ciders.

These fruits, celebrated for their unique flavors and adaptability, were woven into the fabric of medieval cooking and continue to provide a window into the past.

The Medlar

The Medlar fruit has a rich history and folklore in medieval Europe. It was cultivated for over 3,000 years and was native to Iran, southwest Asia, and southeastern Europe, all along the Black Sea coasts from Bulgaria to Turkey. The Romans brought it to England, where it can still be found in many English gardens. The Medlar was transported throughout the warm climates of Europe, where it was grown in palace courtyards, monastery gardens, and village greens.

Medlar fruit is typically not eaten fresh from the tree because it is very tart and astringent when immature. Instead, it is traditionally harvested and allowed to ripen or "blet" off the tree. During this process, the fruit softens and develops its characteristic sweet and spicy taste, somewhat resembling a spiced apple or pear. Once bletted, Medlar fruit can be consumed fresh, used in jams, jellies, or baked into pies and tarts.

Medlar fruit has made appearances in literature, including Shakespearean plays like "Romeo and Juliet," where it was humorously referred to as "open-arse" due to its appearance when ripe.

The Medlar fruit is said to taste a little like apples with a hint of cinnamon. It was highly popular in the Middle Ages, a time when it was known as the "open-arse" fruit due to its appearance when it is ripe. The fruit is harvested when it is still hard and then left to ripen until it becomes soft and brown. This process is called "bletting" and is necessary for the fruit to become edible. The Medlar was used in a variety of dishes, including pies, tarts, and jellies.

The Medlar fruit has also been associated with folklore and superstition. In medieval times, it was believed that the Medlar could cure a broken heart. It was also believed to have magical properties and was used in love potions. In Shakespeare's Romeo and Juliet, the nurse refers to the Medlar as a symbol of love and sexual desire. The Medlar was also believed to have medicinal properties and was used to treat digestive problems, respiratory infections, and menstrual cramps.

In conclusion, the Medlar fruit was a popular fruit in medieval Europe, where it was grown in palace courtyards, monastery gardens, and village greens. It was highly popular in the Middle Ages and was used in a variety of dishes, including pies, tarts, and jellies. The Medlar fruit has also been associated with folklore and superstition, and was believed to have magical properties and was used in love potions. It was also believed to have medicinal properties and was used to treat digestive problems, respiratory infections, and menstrual cramps.

The Medlar fruit was highly popular in medieval Europe, but it has become less popular over time. Here are some reasons why:

1. Difficult to eat
The Medlar fruit is difficult to eat because it needs to be bletted, or left to ripen until it becomes soft and brown, before it can be consumed. This process can

take several weeks, and the fruit can only be eaten when it is fully ripe[1]. This made the fruit less appealing to people who were looking for quick and easy snacks.

2. Unattractive appearance
The Medlar fruit has a unique appearance that some people find unappealing. When it is ripe, it looks like a brown, mushy apple with a large, open calyx at one end[1]. This appearance may have made the fruit less appealing to people who were looking for attractive and visually appealing fruits.

3. Availability
The Medlar fruit is not widely available in supermarkets or grocery stores, which may have contributed to its decline in popularity[3]. It is also not commonly grown in home gardens, which may have made it less accessible to people who were interested in growing their own fruits.

4. Competition from other fruits
As other fruits became more widely available and popular, the Medlar fruit may have lost its appeal[3]. People may have preferred fruits that were easier to eat, more visually appealing, or more widely available.

The Medlar fruit was highly popular in medieval Europe, but it has become less popular over time. The fruit's difficult-to-eat nature, unattractive appearance, limited availability, and competition from other fruits may have contributed to its decline in popularity. However, as people become more interested in heirloom fruits and vegetables, interest in the Medlar fruit is growing again.

The Crab Apple Replacement?

Crab apples were an essential part of medieval European orchards. They were used not only for their fruit but also for their ornamental value.

Crab apples can be an excellent replacement for Medlar in recipes, particularly in culinary applications where the tartness and astringency of Medlar are desired. Here's more information on using crab apples as a substitute:

1. Taste Profile: Like Medlar, crab apples have a tart and astringent taste when raw. This makes them suitable for recipes that require a sour or tangy component.

2. Cooking and Preserving: Crab apples can be used in a variety of culinary applications. They can be cooked down into jams, jellies, and preserves, similar to Medlar. Cooking crab apples with sugar can help mellow their tartness and bring out their natural sweetness.

3. Pies and Tarts: Crab apples work well in pies and tarts, especially when combined with sugar and spices like cinnamon and nutmeg. Their tartness can provide a delightful contrast to sweet pastry or filling.

4. Sauces: Crab apples can be pureed and used as a sauce or condiment to accompany meats or desserts. Their tartness can balance the flavors in savory dishes.

5. Cider and Beverages: Crab apples are sometimes used to make cider or added to fruit juices for their tartness and unique flavor.

6. Preservation: Crab apples can also be preserved in vinegar or pickled for a tangy condiment similar to pickled Medlar.

7. Texture: Depending on the variety and ripeness of crab apples, they may have a slightly firmer texture compared to Medlar, which can be an advantage in recipes where a bit of crunch is desired.

When using crab apples as a substitute for Medlar, it's important to taste and adjust the level of sweetness and spices to match the specific recipe. Additionally, the choice of crab apple variety can impact the overall flavor and texture, so experimenting with different types can help achieve the desired results in your culinary creations.

Crab apples offer a wonderful tartness and versatility in the kitchen, making them a valuable substitute for Medlar in a wide range of recipes. Their natural pectin content and unique flavor make them an excellent choice for jams, pies, sauces, and more, allowing you to explore and create delicious culinary creations.

Experiment with spices like cinnamon, nutmeg, or cloves, and adjust the level of sweetness with sugar, honey, or maple syrup to balance the tartness of the crab apples.

When using crab apples in recipes, remove the core and seeds, as these can be bitter. The skins can usually be left on, but you may choose to peel them if you prefer a smoother texture.

Crab apple trees are often used in orchards to attract pollinators, including bees. They help increase fruit yields in nearby apple and fruit tree varieties.

There are numerous crab apple varieties, each with its unique flavor and appearance. Some produce small, cherry-sized fruit, while others have slightly larger fruit. There are numerous crab apple varieties, each with its unique characteristics, including variations in fruit size, color, and flavor. This diversity makes crab apples a fascinating and versatile group of fruit trees for culinary and ornamental purposes.

In some cultures, crab apples have been associated with symbolism and folklore. For example, in Celtic traditions, crab apples were sometimes considered sacred. In fact, there is a longstanding tradition of planting crabapple trees near homes for protection. These trees were believed to be inhabited by fairies, and they were seen as guardians against negative spirits. In traditional Chinese folklore, crabapple trees were associated with protection, and their blossoms were sometimes used to ward off negative energy.

Crab apples, as much as I love them, are not as common as they used to be. Every Reader needs to fix this one. Plant a crab apple tree.

That being said, if you are unable to find crab apples and medlar fruit, there are a few substitutes that you can use in recipes that call for it. Here are some options:

1. Persimmon
Persimmons have a similar texture and sweetness to medlar fruit, making them a good substitute in recipes. They are also in season during the same time of year as medlar fruit.

Persimmons, native to Asia, were introduced to medieval Europe through trade routes. Initially prized for their exoticism, these sweet fruits gained popularity in royal feasts and courtly banquets. They symbolized luxury and were used in various dishes, contributing to the evolution of medieval European cuisine.

2. Apple
Apples have a similar texture and flavor to medlar fruit, although they are not as sweet. They can be used as a substitute in recipes that call for medlar fruit.

3. Quince
Quinces have a similar texture and flavor to medlar fruit, although they are not as sweet. They can be used as a substitute in recipes that call for medlar fruit.

Quince was sometimes associated with love and fertility in medieval literature. It appeared in romantic stories and legends, including the famous medieval tale of "Sir Gawain and the Green Knight."

4. Pears
Pears have a similar texture and flavor to medlar fruit, although they are not as sweet. They can be used as a substitute in recipes that call for medlar fruit.

In medieval Europe, pears were highly regarded and cultivated in orchards. A true story involves the pear tree at St. Remy Abbey in France. Planted in the 9th century, it survived for over a millennium, bearing fruit until its demise in 2010. This ancient pear tree witnessed centuries of history, including wars, plagues, and changing dynasties, making it a living symbol of endurance and continuity.

5. Rose hips
Rose hips have a similar appearance to medlar fruit, although they are not as sweet. They can be used as a substitute in recipes that call for medlar fruit. Think I'll write a book about RoseHips at some point.

If you are unable to find medlar fruit, there are several substitutes that you can use in recipes that call for it. Persimmons, apples, quinces, pears, and rose hips are all good options.

Growing Fruit Trees

For a first-time fruit tree grower, it's essential to select fruit tree varieties suitable for your climate and location. Medlar trees thrive in temperate climates with well-drained soil and benefit from proper spacing, pruning, and occasional watering. Be aware of the bletting process to harvest the fruit.

Medlar fruit, when harvested, is firm and inedible, often having a tart and astringent taste. To make medlar fruit palatable, it must go through the bletting process, which typically involves a few weeks of storage at cool temperatures. During this time, the fruit's flesh softens, becomes mushy, and takes on a unique flavor and aroma, often described as a combination of apple, pear, and spices. Bletted medlar fruit is typically consumed by spreading the soft, brownish pulp on bread or using it in culinary preparations. The bletting process is essential for transforming these fruits into a delicious and edible treat.

Crabapple trees, on the other hand, are versatile and can adapt to different climates. Plant them in full sun to partial shade with proper spacing and perform regular pruning to maintain shape and health. Pay attention to pest and disease control for both trees and practice good garden hygiene. Enjoy the unique flavors and blossoms that these trees offer, and remember that patience and care are key to successful fruit tree cultivation.

Medlar Fruit Recipes

Medlar Tart

A Medlar tart is a delectable dessert that features bletted Medlar fruit, known for its unique combination of flavors reminiscent of apple and pear. The bletted Medlars are typically incorporated into a sweet pastry crust, creating a delightful tart that captures the distinctive taste of these ancient fruits.

Ingredients

- 500 g Medlar fruit, bletted or 500g of Crabapples
- 1 sheet of shortcrust pastry
- 100 g caster sugar
- 2 eggs
- 100 ml double cream
- 1 tsp ground cinnamon
- 1/2 tsp ground nutmeg
- 1/4 tsp ground cloves

Instructions
1. Preheat the oven to 180°C.
2. Roll out the shortcrust pastry and line a 20 cm tart tin.
3. Prick the base with a fork and bake for 10 minutes.
4. Remove from the oven and let cool.
5. In a bowl, beat the eggs and sugar together.
6. Add the double cream, cinnamon, nutmeg, and cloves and mix well.
7. Pour the mixture over the pastry base.
8. Arrange the Medlar fruit on top of the mixture.
9. Bake for 30-35 minutes, or until the filling is set.
10. Remove from the oven and let cool.

Medlar Jelly with Spices

Medlar jelly is a sweet and tangy preserve made from bletted Medlar fruit. The fruit's natural high pectin content makes it ideal for setting into a thick, flavorful jelly, often enjoyed as a spread on bread or served with cheese and crackers.

Ingredients

1 kg Medlar fruit, bletted or 1kg of Crabapples
1 kg granulated sugar
1 lemon, juiced
1 cinnamon stick
1 star anise
1/2 tsp ground ginger

Instructions
1. Remove the skin from the Medlar fruit and place them in a large pot.
2. Add enough water to cover the fruit and bring to a boil.
3. Reduce the heat and simmer for 30 minutes, or until the fruit is soft.
4. Remove from heat and let cool.
5. Pass the fruit through a sieve to remove the seeds and skins.
6. Measure the puree and add an equal amount of sugar.
7. Add the lemon juice and spices and stir well.
8. Cook over low heat, stirring constantly, until the mixture thickens and reaches the setting point.
9. Pour the mixture into sterilized jars and let cool.

Medlar and Almond Cake

A Medlar and almond cake is a delightful dessert that combines the unique flavors of bletted Medlar fruit with the nutty richness of almonds. The soft, sweet Medlar fruit is often folded into a moist almond-based cake batter, creating a delightful and slightly exotic treat with a distinct combination of flavors. This cake showcases the charming marriage of the tart, aromatic Medlars with the comforting and earthy notes of almonds, resulting in a dessert that's both visually appealing and palate-pleasing.

Ground almonds were a common ingredient in medieval cooking, often used for their versatile and flavorful qualities. They served as a substitute for or addition to flour in various dishes. Ground almonds were used to thicken and enrich sauces, stews, and soups, adding a creamy and slightly nutty flavor. They also appeared in sweet dishes, like marzipan and almond pastes used for desserts, as well as in almond milk, a dairy substitute. Their use in medieval cuisine contributed to both the texture and taste of a wide range of dishes, from savory to sweet, making them a valuable and adaptable component in historical culinary practices.

Ingredients
- 500 g Medlar fruit, bletted or 500 g of Crabapples
- 200 g ground almonds
- 200 g caster sugar
- 4 eggs
- 1 tsp ground cinnamon
- 1/2 tsp ground nutmeg
- 1/4 tsp ground cloves

Instructions:
1. Preheat the oven to 180°C.
2. Grease a 20 cm cake tin and line with baking paper.
3. In a bowl, beat the eggs and sugar together.
4. Add the ground almonds, cinnamon, nutmeg, and cloves and mix well.
5. Pour the mixture into the cake tin.
6. Arrange the Medlar fruit on top of the mixture.
7. Bake for 45-50 minutes, or until the cake is set.
8. Remove from the oven and let cool.

Medlar and Honey Glazed Ham

Medlar-glazed ham is a unique and flavorful dish that combines the sweet and slightly tangy qualities of Medlar fruit with the savory richness of ham. The glaze is typically prepared by simmering bletted Medlar fruit with sugar and spices until it forms a thick, sweet sauce. This glaze is then brushed over a baked or roasted ham, infusing it with a delightful Medlar flavor. The result is a succulent ham with a beautifully caramelized, Medlar-infused crust, offering a blend of sweet and savory notes that make it a standout dish in both taste and presentation.

Ingredients

- 1 kg cooked ham
- 100 g honey
- 100 g Medlar fruit, bletted
- 1 tsp ground cinnamon
- 1/2 tsp ground nutmeg
- 1/4 tsp ground cloves

Instructions

1. Preheat the oven to 180°C.
2. Score the ham in a diamond pattern.
3. In a bowl, mix together the honey, Medlar fruit, cinnamon, nutmeg, and cloves.
4. Brush the mixture over the ham.
5. Bake for 30-40 minutes, or until the glaze is caramelized.
6. Remove from the oven and let cool.

Medlar and Rosemary Roasted Vegetables

Ingredients:
- 500 g mixed root vegetables (carrots, parsnips, potatoes)
- 100 g Medlar fruit, bletted
- 2 tbsp olive oil
- 1 tbsp honey
- 1 tbsp fresh rosemary, chopped
- Salt and pepper to taste

Instructions:
1. Preheat the oven to 200°C.
2. Peel and chop the root vegetables into bite-sized pieces.
3. In a bowl, mix together the olive oil, honey, rosemary, salt, and pepper.
4. Add the root vegetables and Medlar fruit to the bowl and toss to coat.
5. Spread the vegetables out on a baking tray.
6. Roast for 30-40 minutes, or until the vegetables are tender and caramelized.
7. Remove from the oven and let cool.

Grow the Medlar. Cultivate History.

Have I convinced you?

We should go further on the tree. We should always preserve. The Medlar fruit can be grown in the United States and Europe. Here are some tips:

1. Climate
Medlar fruit trees require a cold winter period to produce fruit, similar to apples. They grow well in USDA hardiness zones 59. They can be grown in most parts of Europe, including the UK, and in southern regions of the United States.

2. Soil
Medlar fruit trees prefer welldrained soil that is rich in organic matter. They can tolerate a range of soil types, including clay, loam, and sandy soils.

3. Sunlight
Medlar fruit trees require full sun for optimal fruit production. They can tolerate partial shade, but this may reduce the fruit crop.

4. Planting
Medlar fruit trees should be planted in the fall or early spring. They should be spaced 1520 feet apart. The planting hole should be twice as wide as the root ball and the same depth. The tree should be planted so that the graft union is above the soil line.

5. Care
Medlar fruit trees require regular watering, especially during dry periods. They should be fertilized in the spring with a balanced fertilizer[6]. Pruning should be done in the winter to remove dead or diseased wood and to shape the tree.

In conclusion, medlar fruit can be grown in the United States and Europe. They require a cold winter period to produce fruit, welldrained soil, full sun, and regular care. With the right conditions, medlar fruit trees can produce a unique and delicious fruit that is perfect for use in a variety of recipes.

§

The Medlar fruit trees require a cold winter period, welldrained soil, full sun, and regular care to grow well in the US and Europe. With the right conditions, medlar fruit trees can produce a unique and delicious fruit that is perfect for use in a variety of recipes.

1. Rare and Exotic Fruit
Medlar fruit is considered a rare and exotic fruit[1]. It is not commonly found in nurseries and catalogs, and very little breeding and selection has been done with the fruit.

2. Small Yield
The yield from a single medlar fruit is not particularly impressive, but the production of fruit per bush is respectable, and that's in its third year.

3. SelfFertile
Medlar trees are supposedly selffertile, which is important for those with limited space].

4. Adaptable to Many Soils
Medlar trees perform best in full sun and are adaptable to many soil types.

5. Symbolic Meaning
According to a blog post on Weavers of Wellbeing, the medlar fruit has a symbolic meaning. The fruit can only be eaten when it starts to go gooey and decay, which is a sign that it is ready to be consumed. This is seen as a message of closure and knowledge, as the fruit represents the end of one cycle and the beginning of another.

6. Spiced Apple Flavor
When ripe, medlar fruit tastes like spiced apple.

7. Open Blossom End
Medlar fruit has a distinct, open blossom end.

8. Few Cultivars
Very little breeding and selection has been done with the medlar fruit, as is apparent from the small number of cultivars known.

9. Ancient Fruit
Medlar is a small tree that's been cultivated for thousands of year].

10. Rotten Fruit
Medlar fruit is sometimes referred to as rotten fruit because it must be bletted, or left to ripen until it becomes soft and brown, before it can be consumed.

Medlar fruit and trees have some interesting and little known facts. Medlar fruit is considered a rare and exotic fruit, has a symbolic meaning, and tastes like spiced apple. Medlar trees are adaptable to many soil types and are selffertile. The fruit must be bletted before it can be consumed, which is why it is sometimes referred to as rotten fruit.

Spiced Apple Cider

Crabapple cider and similar fruit-based beverages have a long history in medieval Europe. While crabapples were indeed used for cider making, it's important to note that traditional alcoholic cider production as we know it today was less common during the medieval period. Instead, these ciders were often fermented through wild yeasts and could vary in alcohol content. Spices were also highly valued during medieval times, and they were used to add flavor to many beverages and dishes. The combination of crabapples and spices in cider is a representation of historical culinary traditions, reflecting the flavors and techniques of the past. These beverages were enjoyed during feasts and celebrations, often served warm, and played a role in the culinary heritage of medieval Europe. This is a non-alcohol version that maintains te Medieval flavour profile.

Ingredients

- 20 crabapples, washed and roughly chopped (include cores and peels)
- 1 cinnamon stick
- 56 cloves
- 12 slices of fresh ginger
- 4 cups of water
- Honey or brown sugar (to taste)

Instructions
1. Place the chopped apples, cinnamon stick, cloves, and ginger in a large pot.
2. Add 4 cups of water and bring it to a boil.
3. Reduce heat, cover, and simmer for about 30-45 minutes until the apples are very soft.
4. Use a potato masher to mash the apples and spices.
5. Strain the mixture through a fine-mesh sieve or cheesecloth into a clean pot.
6. Add honey or brown sugar to taste and warm the cider before serving. Adjust sweetness as needed.
7. Serve hot as a warm, spiced beverage enjoyed in medieval times.

Savory Crabapple and Pork Stew

Ingredients

- 1 lb pork shoulder, diced
- 12 crabapples, peeled, cored, and chopped
- 1 onion, chopped
- 2 cloves of garlic, minced
- 2 cups chicken or vegetable broth
- 1/2 teaspoon ground nutmeg
- Salt and pepper to taste
- Olive oil for cooking

Instructions

1. Heat olive oil in a large pot and brown the diced pork pieces.
2. Remove the pork and set it aside.
3. In the same pot, add chopped onions and garlic. Sauté until they're soft and fragrant.
4. Return the pork to the pot, add chopped apples, nutmeg, salt, and pepper.
5. Pour in the broth and bring to a simmer.
6. Cover and cook for about 1 hour, or until the pork is tender and the flavors meld together.
7. Adjust seasoning as needed and serve this savory stew, reminiscent of medieval meat and fruit dishes.

Vegetarian Options

If you'd like to make a contemporary vegetarian or vegan version of this stew, you can replace the pork with hearty plant-based ingredients. Here are a few alternatives:

Seitan:
Seitan, also known as wheat gluten, has a meaty texture and can be used as a substitute for pork in stews.

Tempeh:
Tempeh is a fermented soybean product that works well in savory dishes like stews, providing protein and a chewy texture.

Mushrooms:
A mix of mushrooms, such as shiitake and oyster mushrooms, can provide a meaty, umami flavor and texture.

Lentils:
Green or brown lentils are an excellent choice for a protein-rich and meatless stew. They hold their shape well during cooking.

Jackfruit:
Young, green jackfruit can be used as a meat substitute due to its fibrous texture and mild taste.

Crabapple Tansy

Crabapple Tansy is a unique and historical dessert that takes its inspiration from traditional medieval cuisine. Tansy, in this context, refers to a sweet and savory custardlike dish that combines the tartness of crabapples with aromatic herbs and spices, creating a delightful blend of flavors. It's a nod to the historical culinary creativity that flourished during the Middle Ages.

Ingredients

   * For the Crabapple Mixture:
- 2 cups crabapples, washed, cored, and chopped
- 1/2 cup sugar
- 1/4 cup water
- 1 teaspoon ground cinnamon
- 1/2 teaspoon ground nutmeg
- Zest of one lemon

   * For the Custard:
- 4 large eggs
- 1/2 cup milk
- 1/4 cup sugar
- 1/4 cup fresh rosemary leaves, finely chopped
- Butter for greasing

Instructions

1. In a saucepan, combine the chopped crabapples, sugar, water, ground cinnamon, ground nutmeg, and lemon zest. Cook over medium heat until the crabapples are soft and have broken down into a chunky sauce. This will take about 15-20 minutes. Set aside to cool.
2. Preheat your oven to 350°F (175°C). Grease a baking dish or individual ramekins with butter.
3. In a mixing bowl, beat the eggs and sugar together until well combined. Stir in the chopped rosemary and milk.
4. Pour the crabapple mixture into the prepared baking dish or ramekins.
5. Carefully ladle the custard mixture over the crabapple layer. You can use a spoon to swirl the custard into the crabapples for a marbled effect.
6. Bake in the preheated oven for about 30-35 minutes or until the custard is set and the top is lightly browned.
7. Once done, remove from the oven and let it cool slightly. Serve warm or at room temperature.

Crabapple Tansy is a delightful blend of sweet, tart, and savory flavors, combining the unique essence of crabapples with the earthy aroma of fresh rosemary. It's a sweet and herby custard that provides a tantalizing and historically inspired dessert experience. Enjoy a slice of the past with this one-of-a-kind treat.

Crabapple Milk Cake

Crabapple Milk Cake is a delightful and unique dessert that beautifully captures the sweet and slightly tart essence of crabapples. This original recipe combines fresh crabapples with a moist and tender cake, resulting in a harmonious blend of flavors and textures. The sliced crabapples add a pleasant fruity bite to every slice, while the moist cake crumb provides a comforting backdrop. The glaze, made from crabapple puree and powdered sugar, imparts an extra layer of sweet and tangy indulgence to this delightful treat. Crabapple Milk Cake is a perfect example of how this under-appreciated fruit can be transformed into a delectable and visually pleasing dessert, making it a unique addition to any dessert menu or special occasion.

Ingredients

* For the Cake:
- 1 cup crabapples, washed, cored, and sliced
- 1 cup allpurpose flour
- 1/2 cup sugar
- 1/4 cup unsalted butter, softened
- 1/4 cup milk
- 1 large egg
- 1 teaspoon baking powder
- 1/2 teaspoon vanilla extract
- Pinch of salt

* For the Glaze:
- 1/2 cup crabapple puree (made by cooking and blending crabapples)
- 1 cup powdered sugar

Instructions

1. Preheat your oven to 350°F (175°C) and grease an 8inch round cake pan.
2. In a mixing bowl, cream the softened butter and sugar together until light and fluffy.
3. Beat in the egg and vanilla extract until well combined.
4. In a separate bowl, whisk together the flour, baking powder, and salt.
5. Gradually add the dry ingredients to the wet mixture, alternating with the milk, until a smooth batter forms.
6. Fold in the sliced crabapples.
7. Pour the batter into the prepared cake pan and smooth the top.
8. Bake in the preheated oven for about 25-30 minutes or until a toothpick inserted into the center comes out clean.
9. While the cake is baking, prepare the glaze. Mix the crabapple puree with powdered sugar until you have a smooth glaze.
10. Once the cake is done and has cooled slightly, drizzle the glaze over the top.
11. Allow the cake to cool completely before serving.

Crabapple Sorbet

Crabapple Sorbet is a refreshing and tangy frozen dessert that embodies the unique flavors of crabapples. This original recipe transforms the tartness of crabapples into a smooth and delightful sorbet with a balanced sweet and sour profile. The addition of lemon juice enhances the fruity brightness. Crabapple Sorbet is perfect for a light and palate-cleansing dessert, especially during the warm months. Its vibrant and zesty notes make it a great palate cleanser between courses at a multi-course meal, particularly before a rich main course. It can also be enjoyed as a standalone dessert or paired with a shortbread cookie for added texture and contrast. Whether as a standalone treat or a complement to other dishes, Crabapple Sorbet brings a burst of unique and refreshing flavors to the table.

Ingredients

- 2 cups crabapples, washed and cored
- 1 cup water
- 3/4 cup sugar
- 1 tablespoon lemon juice

Instructions

1. Place the crabapples in a saucepan with water and bring to a boil. Reduce the heat and simmer for about 15 minutes or until the crabapples are soft and can be easily mashed with a fork.
2. Remove from heat and allow the mixture to cool.
3. Using a blender or food processor, puree the cooked crabapples until smooth.
4. Pass the puree through a finemesh sieve to remove any solids or seeds. You should be left with a smooth crabapple puree.
5. In a separate saucepan, combine the sugar and lemon juice with 1/2 cup of water. Heat until the sugar is completely dissolved, creating a simple syrup.
6. Allow the simple syrup to cool.
7. Combine the crabapple puree with the simple syrup and mix well.
8. Pour the mixture into an ice cream maker and churn according to the manufacturer's instructions.
9. Transfer the churned sorbet to a lidded container and freeze for a few hours or until it's firm enough to scoop.

These recipes showcase the delightful and unique flavors of crabapples in a cake and a refreshing sorbet, allowing you to enjoy this underutilized fruit in creative and delicious ways.

VIII

Medieval Grains

such as spelt, emmer wheat, and barley, differ from contemporary grains primarily in terms of their flavor, nutritional profiles, and historical significance. Medieval grains often have a nuttier, earthier flavor and can be more easily digested by some individuals.

They were also central to the diet during the Middle Ages but have largely been replaced by modern wheat varieties in contemporary agriculture and cuisine due to factors like higher yield and easier processing.

Additionally, medieval grains can offer a connection to historical culinary traditions and add diversity to modern diets, making them a unique and valuable addition to contemporary cooking.

Rediscovering and cultivating medieval grains can contribute to biodiversity and sustainable agriculture. They can be more adaptable to various climates and require fewer inputs like pesticides and fertilizers, making them an eco-friendly choice.

Medieval Grains

Grain played a central role in medieval culinary life, serving as the foundation of the medieval diet throughout Europe. Wheat, barley, rye, and oats were among the most commonly cultivated grains, each offering unique culinary possibilities.

Wheat was highly prized for its versatility, used to make bread, pasta, and porridge. Bread was a staple of the medieval diet, varying in quality from coarse, dark peasant loaves to fine, white bread reserved for the nobility. Barley was another essential grain, often used in soups, stews, and gruels, especially among the lower classes.

Rye and oats were hardier grains that thrived in colder climates, making them essential in northern Europe. Rye bread was common, while oats were used to make porridge, gruel, and oatcakes. These grains provided much-needed sustenance during harsh winters.

Grains were typically ground into flour using hand-powered mills and then mixed with water and yeast to make dough. This dough was left to rise and then baked in communal ovens, yielding a variety of bread and baked goods.

Cereals

During the Middle Ages, cereals were the most important staple food. Wheat was generally more expensive and was consumed by the wealthy, while barley, oats, rye, and millet were consumed by the poor. Rice was a fairly expensive import for most of the Middle Ages and was grown in northern Italy only towards the end of the period. Bread, porridge, gruel, and pasta were common dishes made from these grains. Wheat was common all over Europe, but in colder climates, it was usually unaffordable for the majority population and was associated with the higher classes. The centrality of bread in religious rituals such as the Eucharist meant that it enjoyed an especially high prestige among foodstuffs.

In Wiltshire, England, in the 13th and 14th centuries, wheat, barley, and oats were the three most common crops, with varying percentages of each on different manors. Legumes were planted on up to 8 percent of the common land[2]. In northern France, the most important crops were rye, bread wheat, barley, and oats. Rye is more winterhardy and tolerant of poor soils than wheat, and thus became the dominant crop on many marginal and northernmost European sites[2]. In medieval England, the most abundant grain was bread wheat, although specific recognizable varieties of bread wheat were not specified[3].

The grain hierarchy in the Middle Ages was such that the wealthy consumed wheat, while the poor consumed a mixture of wheat and rye flours known as meslin or maslin bread[4]. Peasants mostly had bread from rye or maslin, which produced a darker and heavier variety of bread. Barley bread was more common in some regions[6].

Grains and Wheat in the Middle Ages

These funny or odd facts about grains and wheat in the Middle Ages highlight the differences between modern and medieval agriculture, as well as the class distinctions that existed in medieval society. While wheat was reserved for the upper class, peasants and serfs had to make do with cheaper grains like rye and barley. The diversity of crops grown in medieval fields was also vastly different from modern monoculture fields. Additionally, the type of soil influenced the crops planted, with sandy soils favoring rye and loess and loamy soils favoring wheat. Finally, people ate all types of weird foods during the Middle Ages, but wheat was still reserved for the upper class.

- Wheat was specifically reserved for the upper class, so if you were a peasant, you were likely eating bread made from cheaper grains like rye, barley, or even millet.

- Medieval fields were much more diverse than modern monoculture fields, with a variety of cereal grains being grown.

- Rye was more winterhardy and tolerant of poor soils than wheat, so it became the dominant crop on many marginal and northernmost European site.

- In the lowlands of the Netherlands and adjacent France, the type of soil influenced the crops planted. On sandy soils, wheat was nearly absent as a crop, with rye planted as a winter crop and oats and barley being the principle springplanted crops.

- Outside of harvest time, serfs and peasants mostly consumed even cheaper breads containing no wheat and instead being made up of rye, barley, or other grains.

- People ate all types of weird foods during the Middle Ages, including snake soup, hedgehog, and even porpoise pie. However, wheat was specifically reserved for the upper class.

Medieval Oat & Beer Bread Recipe

Ingredients

- 1 cup oatmeal (regular, not quick oats)
- 1 cup boiling water
- 1/2 cup warm water (about 110º)
- 2 1/4 teaspoons dry active yeast (1 envelope)
- 2 1/2 cups allpurpose flour
- 2 tablespoons brown sugar
- 1 teaspoon salt
- 1/4 cup beer (odd ingredient)

Instructions:
1. In a large bowl, mix together the oatmeal and boiling water. Let sit for 10 minutes.
2. In a separate bowl, mix together the warm water and yeast. Let sit for 5 minutes.
3. Add the yeast mixture to the oatmeal mixture and stir until combined.
4. Add the flour, brown sugar, salt, and beer. Mix until a dough forms.
5. Knead the dough on a floured surface for 10 minutes.
6. Place the dough in a greased bowl and cover with a damp towel. Let rise in a warm place for 1 hour.
7. Preheat the oven to 375°F.
8. Punch down the dough and shape into a loaf. Place in a greased loaf pan.
9. Bake for 30-35 minutes, or until the bread is golden brown and sounds hollow when tapped.

Medieval Honey & Applesauce Oat Bread Recipe

Medieval Honey & Applesauce Oat Bread is a delightful fusion of flavors and textures, inspired by the culinary traditions of the Middle Ages. This unique recipe combines the hearty qualities of oats with the natural sweetness of applesauce and honey. The oats, both ground and whole, provide a rustic and chewy character to the bread, while the applesauce and honey infuse it with a gentle sweetness and moisture.

As it bakes, the kitchen is filled with the warm, comforting aroma of this ancientinspired creation. Each slice of this bread offers a taste of history, echoing the resourceful and inventive spirit of medieval cooks who crafted nourishing and flavorful loaves from simple ingredients.

Whether enjoyed as a side to a hearty stew or as a standalone treat, Medieval Honey & Applesauce Oat Bread invites us to savor the timeless traditions of the past.

Ingredients

- 2 cups oats (1 cup ground, 1 cup whole)
- 2 cups all-purpose flour
- 1 teaspoon salt
- 2 teaspoons baking powder
- 1/2 cup honey
- 1/2 cup unsweetened applesauce
- 1 cup milk
- 1/4 cup melted butter
- 1 egg

Instructions

1. Preheat your oven to 350°F (175°C). Grease a loaf pan.
2. In a large bowl, mix together the ground oats, all-purpose flour, salt, and baking powder.
3. In a separate bowl, combine the honey, applesauce, milk, melted butter, and egg.
4. Pour the wet mixture into the dry ingredients and stir until just combined.
5. Gently fold in the whole oats.
6. Pour the batter into the prepared loaf pan and spread it evenly.
7. Bake for about 45-55 minutes or until a toothpick inserted into the center comes out clean.
8. Allow the bread to cool in the pan for a few minutes before transferring it to a wire rack to cool completely.

Fortified Barley Bread

This fortified barley bread recipe is inspired by medieval cuisine and uses common ingredients from the Middle Ages, such as barley flour, whole wheat flour, rolled oats, honey, and ale. The addition of chopped walnuts, dried figs, and dates adds a unique twist to the traditional recipe, making it a perfect addition to a grand holiday feast.

Ingredients

- 2 cups barley flour
- 2 cups whole wheat flour
- 1/2 cup rolled oats
- 1/2 cup chopped walnuts
- 1/2 cup chopped dried figs
- 1/2 cup chopped dates
- 1/4 cup honey
- 1/4 cup olive oil
- 1 tablespoon active dry yeast
- 1 teaspoon salt
- 1 1/2 cups warm water
- 1/2 cup dark ale

Instructions
1. In a large bowl, mix together the barley flour, whole wheat flour, rolled oats, chopped walnuts, chopped dried figs, and chopped dates.
2. In a separate bowl, mix together the honey, olive oil, active dry yeast, salt, warm water, and dark ale.
3. Add the wet ingredients to the dry ingredients and stir until a dough forms.
4. Knead the dough on a floured surface for 10 minutes.
5. Place the dough in a greased bowl and cover with a damp towel. Let rise in a warm place for 1 hour.
6. Preheat the oven to 375°F.
7. Punch down the dough and shape into a loaf. Place in a greased loaf pan.
8. Bake for 45-50 minutes, or until the bread is golden brown and sounds hollow when tapped.

Posh Porridge with Fruits and Nuts

This posh porridge recipe is inspired by medieval flavors and uses common ingredients from the Middle Ages, such as quinoa, buckwheat groats, and dried fruits and nuts. The addition of honey, brown sugar, cinnamon, and cardamom adds a unique twist to the traditional recipe, making it a perfect addition to a grand holiday feast.

Medieval porridge, also known as medieval gruel, was a basic and common food during the Middle Ages in Europe. It was a simple meal primarily made from grains cooked in water or milk. The exact ingredients and preparation method varied depending on ingredient availability and specific regions in Europe.

Ingredients

- 1 cup steel cut oats
- 1/2 cup quinoa
- 1/2 cup buckwheat groats
- 1/4 cup chia seeds
- 1/2 cup slivered almonds
- 1/2 cup chopped dried figs
- 1/2 cup chopped dates
- 1/4 cup honey
- 1/4 cup brown sugar
- 1 teaspoon ground cinnamon
- 1/4 teaspoon ground cardamom
- 4 cups water
- 1 cup almond milk
- 1/4 cup cocoa nibs (as garnish)

Instructions

1. In a large pot, combine the steel cut oats, quinoa, buckwheat groats, chia seeds, slivered almonds, chopped dried figs, chopped dates, honey, brown sugar, ground cinnamon, ground cardamom, and water.
2. Bring the mixture to a boil over high heat, then reduce the heat to low and simmer for 20-25 minutes, stirring occasionally, until the porridge is thick and creamy.
3. Stir in the almond milk and cook for an additional 5 minutes.
4. Remove from heat and let cool for a few minutes.
5. Serve the porridge in bowls and garnish with cocoa nibs.

Growing Medieval Grains

Growing medieval grains in your home garden can be a rewarding and educational experience, connecting you with historical agricultural practices and providing you with unique, hearty ingredients. While it is beyond the scope of this Book to provide a complete course in growing heritage grains at home, here are some basic growing steps to review before taking the leap.

Selecting Grains

You can grow several types of medieval grains at home, allowing you to connect with historical agricultural practices and enjoy unique, ancient flavors. Here are some common medieval grains suitable for home cultivation:

1. **Barley (Hordeum vulgare):** Barley was one of the most important grains in medieval Europe. It's well-suited for home gardens and can be used for making bread, porridge, and brewing beer.

2. **Oats (Avena sativa):** Oats are another staple grain from the Middle Ages and can be grown in a home garden. They are used for porridge, oatcakes, and as a source of animal feed.

3. **Spelt (Triticum spelta):** Spelt is an ancient grain that was popular during medieval times. It can be used to make flour for bread and various baked goods.

4. **Emmer Wheat (Triticum dicoccum):** Emmer wheat is a precursor to modern wheat and was commonly grown during the medieval period. It can be used for flour, bread, and pasta.

5. **Einkorn Wheat (Triticum monococcum):** Einkorn is one of the earliest cultivated forms of wheat and can be grown at home for flour and baking.

6. **Rye (Secale cereale):** Rye was a significant grain in medieval Northern Europe. It can be used for making rye bread and is known for its hardiness.

7. **Millet (Panicum miliaceum):** Millet was a minor but nutritious grain in medieval Europe. It can be grown in home gardens and used for porridge or ground into flour.

8. **Buckwheat (Fagopyrum esculentum):** While not technically a grain, buckwheat was used in medieval cooking and can be grown at home. It's used for making pancakes and groats.

When cultivating medieval grains at home, be sure to research the specific needs and growing conditions for each grain type, as they may have varying preferences for soil, climate, and spacing. By growing these grains, you can not only explore historical culinary traditions but also enjoy the unique flavors and textures they bring to your modern-day dishes.

Growing Grains: The Basics

That being said, there are some basic steps that will need to be followed regardless of the grain selected.

Preparing the Soil

Prepare your garden soil with well-drained, loamy soil enriched with organic matter. Grains thrive in soil with good drainage and adequate nutrients.

Planting

Sow the grains in early spring or late winter, depending on your climate. Follow the specific planting instructions for each grain type. Generally, plant the seeds in rows or blocks, leaving enough space between plants to allow for healthy growth.

Watering

Grains need consistent moisture during their growth, especially during the initial stages. Be mindful not to overwater, as this can lead to mold and mildew issues.

Maintenance

Keep the garden free from weeds, which can compete with the grains for nutrients and water. Additionally, consider staking or providing support for tall grain varieties to prevent lodging, where the plants bend or fall over due to their weight.

Harvesting

Harvest the grains when they are fully mature. This timing can vary depending on the type of grain, but it's typically in late summer or early autumn. Harvest when the grains are firm and the stalks have turned golden or brown.

Threshing and Winnowing

After harvest, you'll need to separate the grains from the chaff. This process, called threshing and winnowing, can be done by hand or using simple tools like a flail and a breeze or a fan to separate the lighter chaff from the heavier grains.

Storage

Store your harvested grains in a cool, dry place. Ensure they are well-sealed to prevent moisture and pest damage.

Using Your Grains

The grains you've grown can be used in a variety of culinary applications, from making bread and porridge to brewing beer and distilling spirits. Experiment with historical recipes to fully appreciate the flavors and heritage of these grains.

Here are some ways to use medieval grains in your cooking:

1. Baking Bread: Grind medieval grains like spelt, emmer wheat, or barley into flour and use them to make traditional bread. These grains yield flours with distinct flavors and textures that are perfect for hearty, rustic loaves.

2. Porridge: Cook medieval grains into a warm and filling porridge. Oats, barley, and rye are commonly used for porridge. Top with honey, dried fruits, or nuts for added flavor.

3. Cereals: Create a medieval-inspired cereal by mixing cooked grains with milk or yogurt. Add sweeteners like honey or maple syrup and a sprinkle of spices for a delicious breakfast.

4. Grain Salads: Use cooked medieval grains as a base for salads. Combine them with fresh vegetables, herbs, and a vinaigrette for a nutritious and flavorful dish.

5. Pasta: Make homemade pasta using spelt or emmer wheat flour. These ancient grains lend a unique taste and texture to pasta dishes.

6. Soups and Stews: Add medieval grains to your soups and stews to thicken and enrich them. Barley is particularly well-suited for this purpose.

7. Casseroles: Incorporate cooked medieval grains into casseroles for added texture and nutrition. They work well in both savory and sweet casseroles.

8. Brewing Beer: If you're interested in home-brewing, try using barley to make your own medieval-inspired beer. Barley is a key ingredient in beer production.

9. Pancakes and Crepes: Use buckwheat flour to make traditional pancakes or crepes. Buckwheat adds a nutty flavor and is naturally gluten-free.

10. Desserts: Create desserts like rice pudding or tansy using medieval grains. Barley or rice can be used in rice puddings, while a mix of grains can be used in tansy, a sweet custard.

When using medieval grains in your recipes, explore historical cookbooks or online resources for authentic medieval dishes or adapt modern recipes to incorporate these grains. Experimenting with these grains will not only add a historical dimension to your culinary endeavors but also introduce you to diverse and delightful flavors and textures that you might not find in modern grains.

IX

Seaweed

was harvested and used in medieval gardens. Coastal communities across the world have harvested seaweed and used it on their fields to boost their crops for many centuries. In the channel islands, this practice is known as 'vraicing' and there are still official times when it is permissible to cut and gather seaweed. Seaweed has been used in gardens for thousands of years as a liquid or solid additive. Seaweeds have been used to enrich the agricultural soils that were less fertile or soils near the seafront, for a very long time. Seaweed should be used by all gardeners and allotmenteers to supplement the more traditional manures and fertilizers that we use on our plants. Seaweed is too beneficial to be ignored by plant growers. Seaweed farming or kelp farming is the practice of cultivating and harvesting seaweed. In its simplest form, farmers gather from natural beds, while at the same time, seaweeds are used to produce chemicals that can be used for various industrial, pharmaceutical, or food products.

Seaweed

In some coastal areas, people consumed seaweed as part of their diet. While it was not a staple food, various types of seaweed were occasionally eaten. In Japan, for example, nori (a type of seaweed) was used to wrap sushi and as a seasoning.

Though not widely known during medieval times, alginate, a substance derived from seaweed, has been used in various industrial applications, including the production of dental impressions, in more recent times.

Alginate as a Binder: In medieval bookbinding, some manuscripts used a form of gelatin derived from seaweed (known as agar) as a binding agent for inks and pigments.

Alginate in Textiles: In certain parts of the world, alginate from seaweed was used as a sizing agent for textiles, aiding in dyeing and printing processes.

Medieval Seaweed Stew

Seaweed stew, known as "Soupe aux Algues" in France and "Laverbread" in the UK, boasts rich coastal culinary traditions. In France, particularly in Brittany, seaweed has ancient roots as a staple ingredient, with "Soupe aux Algues" being a celebrated traditional Breton dish featuring various seaweeds, often complemented by potatoes, onions, and seafood. In the UK, especially in Wales, "Laverbread" is a historic Welsh specialty made from edible laver seaweed, harvested from coastal rocky shores, boiled, and often mixed with oatmeal, serving as a versatile dish with cultural significance in Welsh cuisine. Both these coastal regions have embraced seaweed in their culinary heritage, evolving into beloved dishes that continue to be enjoyed for their unique flavors and cultural importance.

Ingredients

- 1 tablespoon olive oil
- 1 onion, chopped
- 2 cloves garlic, minced
- 2 carrots, chopped
- 2 celery stalks, chopped
- 1 potato, chopped
- 1 cup chopped seaweed (such as nori or dulse)
- 4 cups vegetable broth
- 1 teaspoon dried thyme
- 1 teaspoon dried rosemary
- Salt and pepper, to taste
- 1 cup cooked quinoa
- 1/2 cup cooked chickpeas

Instructions
1. In a large pot, heat the olive oil over medium heat.
2. Add the onion and garlic and sauté until fragrant, about 2 minutes.
3. Add the carrots, celery, and potato and sauté for an additional 5 minutes.
4. Add the chopped seaweed, vegetable broth, dried thyme, and dried rosemary. Bring to a boil.
5. Reduce the heat to low and simmer for 20-25 minutes, or until the vegetables are tender.
6. Add the cooked quinoa and chickpeas and simmer for an additional 5 minutes.
7. Season with salt and pepper, to taste.
8. Serve hot.

This seaweed stew recipe is inspired by medieval cuisine and uses common ingredients from the Middle Ages, such as seaweed, vegetables, and herbs. The addition of cooked quinoa and chickpeas adds protein and a unique twist to the traditional recipe, making it a perfect addition to a grand holiday feast.

Medieval Seaweed Salt Spice Blend

When used as a seasoning, a seaweed salt blend imparts a complex flavor profile. The saltiness from the sea salt is complemented by the umami richness of the seaweed, offering a savory, slightly sweet, and oceanic taste. Depending on the seaweed variety used, you may also detect subtle herbal or vegetal notes.

The blend emits a distinctive aroma that combines the brininess of sea salt with earthy, oceanic notes from the dried seaweed. It often has a hint of marine freshness.

And, in keeping with the theme of this Book, our seaweed salt spice blend recipe is inspired by medieval cuisine and uses common ingredients from the Middle Ages, such as seaweed and sea salt. The addition of black pepper, garlic powder, onion powder, paprika, cumin, and ground coriander adds a unique twist to the traditional recipe, making it a perfect addition to any dish.

Ingredients

- 1/4 cup dried seaweed (such as nori or dulse)
- 1/4 cup sea salt
- 1 tablespoon black pepper
- 1 tablespoon garlic powder
- 1 tablespoon onion powder
- 1 tablespoon paprika
- 1 teaspoon cumin
- 1 tablespoon ground coriander

Instructions

1. In a food processor, pulse the dried seaweed until it is finely chopped.
2. In a bowl, mix together the seaweed, sea salt, black pepper, garlic powder, onion powder, paprika, cumin, and ground coriander.
3. Store the spice blend in an airtight container.

X
Honey and Mead

were important commodities in the Middle Ages, with honey being used as a sweetener, a preservative, and a basic ingredient of mead. The cultivation of honey and the production of mead were widespread throughout Europe, and the drink was enjoyed by people of all classes.

Cultivation of Honey

1. Beekeeping: Beekeeping was a common practice in the Middle Ages, and honey was harvested from hives kept in gardens, fields, and forests. Bees were kept in a variety of containers, including woven baskets, hollow logs, and clay pots.

2. Honey Extraction: Honey was extracted from the comb by crushing it or by using a press. The honey was then strained to remove any impurities and stored in jars or barrels.

3. Uses of Honey: Honey was used as a sweetener in a variety of dishes, including bread, cakes, and pastries. It was also used as a preservative for fruits and meats, and as a medicine for a variety of ailments.

Uses of Mead

1. As a Drink: Mead was a popular drink in the Middle Ages and was enjoyed by people of all classes. It was made by fermenting honey mixed with water, and sometimes with added ingredients such as fruits, herbs, or spices.

2. As a Medicine: Mead was also used as a medicine for a variety of ailments, including digestive issues, respiratory problems, and skin conditions.

3. As a Symbol: Mead was often used as a symbol of hospitality and was served at feasts and celebrations. It was also used in religious ceremonies and was believed to have magical properties.

Bees in Medieval Literature

1. Bees in the Bible: Bees are mentioned several times in the Bible, including in the book of Judges, where Samson finds honey in the carcass of a lion.

2. Bees in Literature: Bees were also mentioned in medieval literature, including in the works of Chaucer and Shakespeare. In Chaucer's Canterbury Tales, the character of the Wife of Bath keeps bees and uses honey as a metaphor for sexual pleasure.

Medieval Beekeepers

Medieval beekeepers, known as apiarists, practiced traditional beekeeping methods using skeps, woven straw hives, to house honeybee colonies. They played a vital role in honey production and beeswax harvesting, with honey serving as a valuable sweetener and beeswax having various uses. Beekeeping was seasonal, and beekeepers possessed traditional knowledge, managing hives, and harvesting honey in late summer. Monasteries were often involved in beekeeping, with monks and nuns tending to hives in their gardens for sustenance and medicinal purposes. Beekeeping guilds also regulated the trade, sharing knowledge and establishing quality standards for honey and beeswax. Bees and beekeeping held religious symbolism in medieval Europe, representing diligence and order. These practices, rooted in centuries of tradition, laid the foundation for modern beekeeping, which saw significant advancements in hive design, bee biology understanding, and beekeeping techniques during the 18th and 19th centuries.

3 Books on Beekeeping

1. The Backyard Beekeeper: An Absolute Beginner's Guide to Keeping Bees in Your Yard and Garden by Kim Flottum - This book is a great resource for beginners who are interested in keeping bees in their backyard. It covers the basics of beekeeping, including equipment, hive management, and honey production.

2. The Practical Beekeeper: Beekeeping Naturally by Michael Bush - This book is a comprehensive guide to natural beekeeping, which emphasizes the importance of working with the bees' natural instincts. It covers a wide range of topics, including hive design, swarm management, and disease prevention.

3. Honeybee Democracy by Thomas D. Seeley - This book is a fascinating look at the behavior and decision-making processes of honeybees. It explores how bees make collective decisions and how they communicate with each other to find the best new home for their colony.

These books are highly regarded by beekeepers and provide valuable insights into the world of bees and beekeeping. Whether you are a beginner or an experienced beekeeper, these books are sure to provide valuable information and tips for keeping healthy and productive hives.

Bee-friendly Plants

Bees are attracted to some plants more than others due to factors like flower color, shape, scent, and the quality of nectar and pollen. Bees prefer brightly colored flowers, especially in blue, purple, and yellow hues, with convenient shapes for landing and feeding. Fragrant flowers also entice bees, and the timing of flowering plays a role, as bees forage when certain plants are in bloom. Ultimately, bees prioritize the most rewarding food sources, ensuring effective pollination for both the bees and the plants.Some plants that are particularly attractive to bees include:

- Sunflowers
- Lavender
- Wildflowers
- Daisies
- Coneflowers
- Black-eyed Susans
- Bee balm
- Salvia
- Thyme
- Rosemary

Planting a Bee-Friendly Garden

is a great way to support the health and survival of bees, which are essential pollinators for many of the foods we eat. By providing bees with a variety of food sources, shelter, and water, we can help ensure that they have the resources they need to thrive. Here are some tips for creating a bee-friendly garden:

1. **Choose Native Plants:** Native plants are adapted to the local climate and soil conditions, making them more attractive to bees. Choose a variety of plants that bloom at different times throughout the year to provide bees with a continuous source of food.

2. **Plant a Variety of Flowers:** Bees are attracted to a variety of flowers, including daisies, sunflowers, lavender, and wildflowers. Plant a mix of annuals and perennials to provide bees with a diverse range of food sources.

3. **Avoid Pesticides:** Pesticides can be harmful to bees and other pollinators. Avoid using pesticides in your garden and opt for natural pest control methods instead.

4. **Provide Shelter:** Bees need shelter to protect them from the elements and predators. You can provide shelter by creating a bee hotel or leaving dead wood and hollow stems in your garden.

5. **Offer a Source of Water:** Bees need water to survive, so provide a source of water in your garden, such as a shallow dish filled with water and stones.

6. **Create a Sunny Spot:** Bees are attracted to sunny spots, so choose a location in your garden that gets plenty of sunlight.

7. **Avoid Hybrid Plants:** Hybrid plants may not produce as much nectar or pollen as their non-hybrid counterparts, making them less attractive to bees.

8. **Plant Herbs:** Many herbs, such as basil, thyme, and rosemary, are attractive to bees and can be used in cooking.

9. **Avoid Chemical Fertilizers:** Chemical fertilizers can be harmful to bees and other pollinators. Opt for natural fertilizers, such as compost or manure, instead.

10. **Provide a Variety of Structures:** Bees need a variety of structures to build their nests, including hollow stems, dead wood, and bee hotels.

Oozy Honey Treacle Pie
with Fruit and Medieval Spices, including Saffron

This oozy honey treacle pie with fruit and medieval spices, including saffron, is a delicious and unique twist on the traditional treacle tart. The addition of honey and dried fruit adds sweetness and texture, while the spices, including saffron, add a warm and complex flavor profile that is perfect for a grand holiday feast.

Ingredients

- 1 batch of your favorite pastry crust recipe, mixed, chilled, and rolled out (or a prepared pie crust)
- 1 cup honey
- 1 cup golden syrup
- 1/4 cup heavy cream
- 1 cup bread crumbs
- 1 lemon, zested
- 1/2 cup dried fruit (such as raisins, currants, or chopped apricots)
- 1/2 teaspoon ground cinnamon
- 1/4 teaspoon ground ginger
- 1/4 teaspoon ground nutmeg
- 1/4 teaspoon ground cloves
- 1/4 teaspoon ground saffron

Instructions

1. Preheat the oven to 350°F.
2. Roll out the pastry crust and line a 9inch pie dish.
3. In a saucepan, heat the honey, golden syrup, and heavy cream over medium heat until combined.
4. Stir in the bread crumbs, lemon zest, dried fruit, cinnamon, ginger, nutmeg, cloves, and saffron.
5. Pour the mixture into the prepared pie crust.
6. Bake for 30-35 minutes, or until the filling is set and the crust is golden brown.
7. Let the pie cool for at least 10 minutes before serving.

Making Mead at Home

is a fun and rewarding process that can be done with basic equipment and ingredients. Here is a basic procedure for making mead at home:

1. **Sanitize Your Equipment:** Sanitizing your equipment is important to prevent contamination of your mead. You can use a sanitizing solution or boil your equipment in hot water.

2. **Combine Honey and Water:** Mix honey and water together in a container of choice, whether that be a bucket or demijohn. The ratio of honey to water can vary depending on the desired sweetness and alcohol content of your mead.

3. **Mix The Must:** Stir the honey and water mixture until the honey is fully dissolved. You can also add fruit, spices, or other flavorings at this point.

4. **Check The Specific Gravity:** Use a hydrometer to check the specific gravity of your must. This will give you an idea of the alcohol content of your mead.

5. **Add Your Yeast:** Add your yeast to the must and stir well. There are many different types of yeast that can be used for mead, so choose one that fits your desired flavor profile.

6. **Ferment Your Mead:** Cover your container with a lid or airlock and let your mead ferment for several weeks. The length of fermentation will depend on the type of yeast used and the desired alcohol content of your mead.

7. **Rack Your Mead:** After fermentation is complete, transfer your mead to a new container using a siphon. This will help to clarify your mead and remove any sediment.

8. **Age Your Mead:** Age your mead for several months to allow the flavors to develop. You can age your mead in a bottle or a barrel, depending on your preference.

9. **Bottle Your Mead:** Once your mead has aged, it is ready to be bottled. Use sanitized bottles and corks or caps to store your mead.

10. **Enjoy Your Mead:** Your mead is now ready to be enjoyed! Serve it chilled or at room temperature, depending on your preference.

Making mead at home is a simple and rewarding process that can be customized to your taste preferences. With basic equipment and ingredients, you can create a delicious and unique beverage that has been enjoyed for centuries.

Reading Mead

Here are two recommended books on making mead at home:

1. The Complete Guide to Making Mead: The Ingredients, Equipment, Processes, and Recipes for Crafting Honey Wine by Steve Piatz

This book is considered one of the best resources for making mead at home. It covers everything from the history of mead to the equipment needed to make it, and includes a variety of recipes for different types of mead.

2. The Compleat Meadmaker: Home Production of Honey Wine From Your First Batch to Award-winning Fruit and Herb Variations by Ken Schramm

This book is another highly recommended resource for making mead at home. It covers the basics of mead making, as well as more advanced techniques for creating unique and flavorful meads. It also includes a variety of recipes and tips for aging and bottling your mead.

Both of these books are highly regarded by the mead making community and provide comprehensive information on the process of making mead at home. Whether you are a beginner or an experienced mead maker, these books are sure to provide valuable insights and tips for creating delicious and unique meads.

Mead Bread Pudding with Currants

This mead bread pudding with currants is a delicious and unique twist on the traditional bread pudding. The addition of mead and currants adds sweetness and depth of flavor, while the spices add a warm and complex flavor profile that is perfect for a cozy fall or winter dessert. Serve warm with a dollop of whipped cream or a drizzle of honey for an extra special treat.

Ingredients

- 6 cups of cubed bread (stale or toasted)
- 4 eggs
- 2 cups of milk
- 1 cup of mead
- 1/2 cup of honey
- 1/2 cup of dried currants
- 1 teaspoon of ground cinnamon
- 1/2 teaspoon of ground nutmeg
- 1/4 teaspoon of ground cloves
- 1/4 teaspoon of salt

Instructions:

1. Preheat the oven to 350°F.
2. Grease a 9x13 inch baking dish.
3. In a large mixing bowl, whisk together the eggs, milk, mead, honey, cinnamon, nutmeg, cloves, and salt.
4. Add the cubed bread and currants to the bowl and mix well.
5. Let the mixture sit for 10-15 minutes to allow the bread to soak up the liquid.
6. Pour the mixture into the prepared baking dish.
7. Bake for 40-45 minutes, or until the top is golden brown and the pudding is set.
8. Let the pudding cool for 10-15 minutes before serving.

XI

Saffron was a medieval spice. It was highly prized in medieval Europe and was used in a variety of dishes, including sweet and savory dishes.

- Saffron was a prized spice in the Medieval cookery of Italy, Catalonia, and England.

- Both saffron and the crocus from which it comes were well-traveled during the Middle Ages, and as of the fourteenth century, there were Saffron.

- Saffron was used by medieval monks mixed with egg white to substitute for gold leaf in illuminated manuscripts.

- Saffron was neglected in Europe from the 5th century CE but was reintroduced to Spain by the Arabs in the 10th century and gained esteem in the cuisine of the Middle Ages and the Renaissance.

- Saffron was an article of long-distance trade before Crete's Minoan palace culture reached.

- Saffron was front and center at royal banquets in medieval times.

Wild Boar with Saffron with Medieval Spices

This recipe showcases the harmonious combination of wild game meat and the luxurious saffron spice, resulting in a flavorful and aromatic dish that reflects the culinary heritage of medieval Europe. Wild Boar with Saffron is not only a delicious meal but also a testament to the historical and cultural significance of these ingredients in traditional European cuisine.

Ingredients

- 2 lbs wild boar meat, cut into chunks
- 1 onion, chopped
- 2 cloves garlic, minced
- 1 cup red wine
- 1/2 cup honey
- 1/4 cup garum (fish sauce)
- 1/4 cup olive oil
- 1/2 teaspoon ground cinnamon
- 1/4 teaspoon ground ginger
- 1/4 teaspoon ground nutmeg
- 1/4 teaspoon ground cloves
- 1/4 teaspoon ground saffron
- Salt and pepper, to taste

Instructions

1. Preheat the oven to 350°F.
2. In a large Dutch oven or ovensafe pot, heat the olive oil over medium-high heat.
3. Add the onion and garlic and sauté until softened, about 5 minutes.
4. Add the wild boar meat and brown on all sides, about 10 minutes.
5. Add the red wine, honey, garum, cinnamon, ginger, nutmeg, cloves, saffron, salt, and pepper.
6. Bring the mixture to a simmer and then cover the pot with a lid.
7. Transfer the pot to the oven and bake for 2-3 hours, or until the meat is tender and falling apart.
8. Serve the wild boar with saffron hot, garnished with fresh herbs if desired.

Wild Boar

Wild boar was a highly sought-after source of food during medieval times in Europe, catering to both the nobility and common people. The pursuit of wild boars was not merely a means of sustenance but a revered pastime among the medieval elite, often intertwined with chivalric traditions and displays of hunting prowess. The meat of the wild boar was prized for its exceptional flavor and tenderness, considered a culinary delicacy. It could be prepared in a variety of ways, such as roasting on an open spit, slow-cooked to perfection, or marinated and seasoned with a rich array of herbs and spices. Wild boar meat graced the tables of grand feasts and celebrations, symbolizing opulence and abundance, and was especially prominent during festive occasions like Christmas. Culinary manuscripts from the Middle Ages contained numerous recipes showcasing the versatility of wild boar in medieval cuisine, often utilizing ingredients like honey, vinegar, and spices to create complex and flavorful dishes. Beyond its culinary significance, the wild boar also held cultural and symbolic importance, occasionally representing courage and valor in medieval literature and heraldry. In sum, wild boar was a central and celebrated element of medieval gastronomy, leaving an indelible mark on the culinary traditions of the era.

Three Side Dishes for Wild Boar

Roasted Root Vegetables

Medieval Roasted Root Vegetables were a staple of medieval European cuisine, particularly during the colder months when fresh produce was limited. This dish is a testament to the simplicity and practicality of medieval cooking, as well as the use of locally available ingredients

Ingredients:
- 2 lbs mixed root vegetables (such as carrots, parsnips, and turnips), peeled and chopped
- 2 tablespoons olive oil
- Salt and pepper, to taste

Instructions:

1. Preheat the oven to 400°F.
2. Toss the chopped root vegetables with olive oil, salt, and pepper.
3. Spread the vegetables out on a baking sheet and roast for 30-40 minutes, or until tender and golden brown.

Saffron Rice

Saffron rice, during medieval times, was a prized and luxurious dish that showcased the opulence and sophistication of medieval feasts.

Rice, itself, was primarily used in high cuisine, particularly in the courts of medieval Europe.

Ingredients:
- 2 cups white rice
- 4 cups water
- 1/4 teaspoon ground saffron
- Salt and pepper, to taste
-

Instructions:

1. Rinse the rice in cold water and drain.
2. In a large pot, bring the water to a boil.
3. Add the rice, saffron, salt, and pepper.
4. Reduce the heat to low and cover the pot with a lid.
5. Simmer the rice for 18-20 minutes, or until the water is absorbed and the rice is tender.

Honey-Glazed Carrots

One interesting anecdote about carrots in medieval times involves the perception of this humble root vegetable. Contrary to the modern vibrant orange carrots we're accustomed to, medieval carrots were often purple, red, white, or yellow in color. The orange carrot we know today is the result of selective breeding in the Netherlands during the 17th century, specifically in tribute to the Dutch Royal House of Orange.

In medieval Europe, carrots were not as widely cultivated as they are now, and the carrot varieties in use had a somewhat different appearance and taste. Purple and yellow carrots, for example, were more common. The orange carrot, when it appeared, was initially seen as a novelty and a luxury due to its vibrant color, which was associated with wealth and prestige. Over time, the orange carrot gained popularity and became the norm, while the older, differently colored varieties faded into obscurity.

A cautionary note: while the story of orange carrots being developed as a tribute to the Dutch Royal House of Orange is a widely circulated anecdote, its historical accuracy should be viewed with some skepticism, as it may oversimplify a more intricate agricultural history.

Ingredients:
- 1 lb carrots, peeled and sliced
- 2 tablespoons butter
- 2 tablespoons honey
- Salt and pepper, to taste

Instructions:

1. In a large skillet, melt the butter over medium heat.
2. Add the sliced carrots and sauté for 5-7 minutes, or until tender.
3. Drizzle the honey over the carrots and stir to coat.
4. Season with salt and pepper to taste.

§

The wild boar with saffron recipe with medieval spices and three side dishes is a delicious and hearty meal that is perfect for a special occasion or holiday feast. The saffron adds a warm and complex flavor profile to the wild boar, while the side dishes provide a variety of textures and flavors to complement the meat. By incorporating saffron and other medieval spices into your cooking, you can create a unique and flavorful meal that pays homage to the rich culinary history of the Middle Ages.

XII

Two Elaborate Digestifs
to End the Food and Drink Section of the Book

Saffron and Honey Old Fashioned with Aged Rum and Saffron Salt Rim

This saffron and honey Old Fashioned with aged rum and saffron salt rim is a sophisticated and unique cocktail that is sure to impress. The saffron honey syrup adds a warm and complex flavor profile to the aged rum, while the saffron salt rim adds a touch of medieval flavor. By incorporating saffron and honey into your cocktails, you can add a unique and flavorful twist to a classic cocktail.

Ingredients

- 2 oz aged rum (such as Kirk & Sweeney 23)
- 1/4 oz saffron honey syrup (made by combining 1/2 cup honey, 1/4 teaspoon ground saffron, and 1/4 cup water in a saucepan and simmering until the honey is dissolved)
- 2 dashes orange bitters
- Saffron salt (made by combining 1/4 teaspoon ground saffron and 1/4 cup sea salt)
- Orange peel, for garnish

Instructions
1. Rim a rocks glass with saffron salt.
2. In a mixing glass, combine the aged rum, saffron honey syrup, and orange bitters.
3. Fill the glass with ice and stir until well chilled.
4. Strain the mixture into the salt-rimmed rocks glass filled with ice.
5. Garnish with an orange peel.
6. Serve the saffron and honey Old Fashioned cold.

Saffron and Honey Liqueur Sour with Yellow Chartreuse Cocktail

This saffron and honey liqueur sour with yellow Chartreuse cocktail is a complex and elegant drink that is perfect for a special occasion. The saffron and honey liqueur adds a warm and floral flavor profile to the cocktail, while the yellow Chartreuse and Luxardo Maraschino Liqueur add a touch of herbal and bitter notes. The egg white gives the cocktail a frothy and silky texture. By incorporating saffron and honey into your cocktails, you can add a unique and flavorful twist to a classic cocktail.

Ingredients

- 2 oz saffron and honey liqueur
- 1 oz lemon juice
- 1/2 oz yellow Chartreuse
- 1/2 oz Luxardo Maraschino Liqueur
- Egg white
- Saffron threads, for garnish

Instructions
1. In a shaker filled with ice, combine the saffron and honey liqueur, lemon juice, yellow Chartreuse, Luxardo Maraschino Liqueur, and egg white.
2. Shake well and strain the mixture into a coupe glass.
3. Garnish with a few saffron threads.
4. Serve the saffron and honey liqueur sour cold.

About Chartreuse

The history of Chartreuse begins in 1084 when Saint Bruno of Cologne founded the Carthusian Order in the Chartreuse Mountains near Grenoble, France. The order was known for its strict vows of silence and contemplative way of life.

In 1605, the Carthusian monks at the Grande Chartreuse monastery received a manuscript from a French marshal, François Annibal d'Estrées, containing a recipe for an herbal elixir. It was said to be a gift from the marshal for their healing skills. The elixir was called "Elixir Végétal de la Grande Chartreuse."

The monks began producing the elixir for medicinal purposes. Over time, they refined the recipe and turned it into a liqueur known as "Chartreuse." The recipe included a complex blend of 130 different herbs, plants, and flowers, with its exact formulation known only to a few monks.

XIII
Final Words on the Medieval Garden

The Influence of Medieval Gardens

The influence of medieval gardens on Renaissance, European, UK, and US gardens and garden design is significant and long-lasting. Medieval gardens were orderly spaces where beauty coexisted with utility. Gardeners of the Middle Ages developed essential skills and learned to grow edible, medicinal, and decorative plants that are still indispensable to us today. In this article, we will explore the lasting influences of medieval gardens on garden design in the Renaissance, Europe, the UK, and the US, and provide examples of gardens that demonstrate this influence.

Medieval Gardens and Renaissance Garden Design
Medieval gardens lacked many of the features of the Renaissance gardens that followed them, but some of the characteristics of these gardens continue to be seen in modern garden design. The Renaissance garden was dominated by the Italian garden, which developed into the French formal garden, dominating the Baroque period. Both were formal styles, attempting to impose architectural principles on the garden. The Italian garden was characterized by its use of symmetry, axial planning, and water features. The French formal garden was characterized by its use of parterres, topiary, and fountains. These formal styles were a reaction to the informality of medieval gardens, which were seen as wild and uncontrolled.

One of the most famous examples of Renaissance garden design is the Villa d'Este in Tivoli, Italy. The villa was built in the 16th century for Cardinal Ippolito II d'Este, and the gardens were designed by Pirro Ligorio. The gardens are characterized by their use of water features, including fountains, cascades, and waterfalls. The garden is also known for its use of topiary, grottoes, and parterres.

Medieval Gardens and European Garden Design
In Europe, the formal garden à la française, exemplified by the Gardens of Versailles, became the dominant horticultural style until the middle of the 18th century when the English landscape garden and the French landscape garden acceded to dominance. The English landscape garden was apparently informal and natural, but required very large spaces, and by the end of the century dominated all Europe in the largest new gardens. The French landscape garden was characterized by its use of naturalistic planting, winding paths, and water features.

One of the most famous examples of European garden design is the Gardens of Versailles in France. The gardens were designed by André Le Nôtre in the 17th century for Louis XIV. The gardens are characterized by their use of parterres, topiary, and fountains. The gardens also feature a large canal, which was used for boating and other water activities.

Medieval Gardens and UK Garden Design
In the UK, the English landscape garden developed in the 18th century. The English landscape garden was characterized by its use of naturalistic planting, winding paths, and water features. The English landscape garden was a reaction to the formal gardens of the Baroque period, which were seen as artificial and contrived. The English landscape garden was also influenced by the Romantic movement, which emphasized the beauty of nature.

One of the most famous examples of UK garden design is Stourhead in Wiltshire. The garden was designed by Henry Hoare II in the 18th century and is characterized by its use of naturalistic planting, winding paths, and water features. The garden features a large lake, which is surrounded by trees and shrubs. The garden also features a number of classical temples and other architectural features.

Medieval Gardens and US Garden Design
In the US, the influence of medieval gardens can be seen in the use of naturalistic planting and water features. The US has a long tradition of landscape gardening, which dates back to the 19th century. The US landscape gardening movement was influenced by the English landscape garden and the Romantic movement.

One of the most famous examples of US garden design is Central Park in New York City. The park was designed by Frederick Law Olmsted and Calvert Vaux in the 19th century and is characterized by its use of naturalistic planting, winding paths, and water features. The park features a large lake, which is surrounded by trees and shrubs. The park also features a number of architectural features, including bridges, arches, and fountains.

Conclusion
The influence of medieval gardens on garden design in the Renaissance, Europe, the UK, and the US is significant and long-lasting. Medieval gardens were orderly spaces where beauty coexisted with utility, and gardeners of the Middle Ages developed essential skills and learned to grow edible, medicinal, and decorative plants that are still indispensable to us today. The formal styles of the Renaissance and Baroque periods were a reaction to the informality of medieval gardens, and the English landscape garden was a reaction to the formal gardens of the Baroque period. The influence of medieval gardens can be seen in the use of naturalistic planting and water features in garden design today. Examples of gardens that demonstrate this influence include the Villa d'Este in Tivoli, the Gardens of Versailles, Stourhead, and Central Park.

The Influence of Medieval Cuisine

Medieval cuisine has had a lasting influence on modern cuisine in France, Spain, the UK, Germany, Italy, and the US. The Middle Ages lasted from the fifth to the fifteenth century, and during this period, diets and cooking changed less than they did in the early modern period that followed, when those changes helped lay the foundations for modern European cuisines[2]. Here are some examples of how medieval cuisine has influenced modern cuisine in different countries:

France
Medieval French cuisine was characterized by its use of spices, such as cinnamon, cloves, and ginger, and its emphasis on meat dishes. The French also developed a taste for wine, which remains a staple of French cuisine today. The cuisine of southern France had far more in common with Italian and Spanish cooking than with northern French cuisine[1]. French cuisine has continued to evolve, but it still retains many of the characteristics of medieval French cuisine. For example, French cuisine still emphasizes the use of fresh, high-quality ingredients, and it still relies heavily on meat dishes.

Spain
Medieval Spanish cuisine was influenced by the Moors, who introduced new ingredients and cooking techniques to Spain. The Moors introduced rice, almonds, and saffron to Spain, which are still staples of Spanish cuisine today. The Spanish also developed a taste for wine, which remains an important part of Spanish cuisine. Spanish cuisine has continued to evolve, but it still retains many of the characteristics of medieval Spanish cuisine. For example, Spanish cuisine still emphasizes the use of fresh, high-quality ingredients, and it still relies heavily on rice dishes.

UK
Medieval British cuisine was characterized by its use of simple ingredients, such as meat, vegetables, and grains. The level of refinement was low, and international influence was fairly insignificant. This all changed in the 11th century after the Norman invasion. With the invaders came a new and less provincial gentry, and new eating habits, especially for the nobility. While traditional British cooking today is not regarded with high esteem internationally, the Medieval Anglo-Norman cooks were considerably more refined and more cosmopolitan[1]. The UK has continued to develop its cuisine, but it still retains many of the characteristics of medieval British cuisine. For example, British cuisine still emphasizes the use of simple, high-quality ingredients, and it still relies heavily on meat dishes.

Germany
Medieval German cuisine was characterized by its use of simple ingredients, such as meat, vegetables, and grains. The Germans also developed a taste for beer, which remains an important part of German cuisine. German cuisine has

continued to evolve, but it still retains many of the characteristics of medieval German cuisine. For example, German cuisine still emphasizes the use of simple, high-quality ingredients, and it still relies heavily on meat dishes.

Italy

Medieval Italian cuisine was characterized by its use of new ingredients and spices, such as pepper and cinnamon, which allowed Italians to try new dishes. Invading nations brought their own culinary influences, which also impacted the foods people in Italy could eat and how they prepared their meals. The rise of Christianity during the Middle Ages influenced what was considered acceptable to eat, and the Church imposed new rules about what people should eat. Meat became associated with luxury and was reserved for special occasions[5]. Italian cuisine has continued to evolve, but it still retains many of the characteristics of medieval Italian cuisine. For example, Italian cuisine still emphasizes the use of fresh, high-quality ingredients, and it still relies heavily on pasta dishes.

US

Medieval cuisine has also influenced modern cuisine in the US. The US has a long tradition of cuisine that dates back to the 19th century. The US cuisine was influenced by the English landscape garden and the Romantic movement. The US cuisine still emphasizes the use of fresh, high-quality ingredients, and it still relies heavily on meat dishes. The US cuisine has continued to evolve, but it still retains many of the characteristics of medieval cuisine[2].

Examples of Medieval-Influenced Gardens

There are many gardens that demonstrate the influence of medieval gardens on modern garden design. Here are some examples:

The Cloisters in New York City is a museum that features medieval art and architecture. The gardens at The Cloisters are designed to evoke the feeling of a medieval garden, with their use of herbs, flowers, and water features.

The Garden of Cosmic Speculation in Scotland is a modern garden that is inspired by medieval gardens. The garden features a labyrinth, a water garden, and a Chinese garden, all of which are designed to evoke the feeling of a medieval garden.

The Garden of the Villa Gamberaia in Tuscany, Italy, is a Renaissance garden that is inspired by medieval gardens. The garden features a water garden, a parterre, and a grotto, all of which are designed to evoke the feeling of a medieval garden.

The Garden of the Alhambra in Granada, Spain, is a medieval garden that is inspired by Islamic gardens. The garden features a water garden, a courtyard, and a pavilion, all of which are designed to evoke the feeling of a medieval garden.

The Garden of the Château de Villandry in France is a Renaissance garden that is inspired by medieval gardens. The garden features a water garden, a parterre, and a maze, all of which are designed to evoke the feeling of a medieval garden.

In conclusion, medieval cuisine has had a lasting influence on modern cuisine in France, Spain, the UK, Germany, Italy, and the US. The characteristics of medieval cuisine, such as the use of fresh, high-quality ingredients and the reliance on meat dishes, can still be seen in modern cuisine. Medieval gardens have also influenced modern garden design, with their use of herbs, flowers, and water features. Examples of gardens that demonstrate this influence include The Cloisters, The Garden of Cosmic Speculation, The Garden of the Villa Gamberaia, The Garden of the Alhambra, and The Garden of the Château de Villandry.

Final Thoughts on Medieval Gardens

Medieval gardens were orderly spaces where beauty coexisted with utility. Gardeners of the Middle Ages developed essential skills and learned to grow edible, medicinal, and decorative plants that are still indispensable to us today. The medieval garden is a metaphor for the human condition, providing solace and reflection, and a source of inspiration and cultural foundation that can be shared by the world, regardless of their professions, hobbies, nationality, or religion. Chefs, gardeners, scholars, culture hounds, gourmands, travelers, researchers, builders, and writers all find a place in the medieval garden, both in real life and its far-reaching, ever-expanding influences.

The medieval garden is a reflection of the human condition, as it combines beauty and utility. The gardeners of the Middle Ages developed essential skills and learned to grow edible, medicinal, and decorative plants that are still indispensable to us today. The medieval garden provides a source of solace and reflection, as it is a place where one can escape from the hustle and bustle of daily life and connect with nature. The garden also provides a source of inspiration and cultural foundation that can be shared by the world, regardless of their professions, hobbies, nationality, or religion.

Chefs find a place in the medieval garden, as they can use the herbs, fruits, and vegetables grown in the garden to create delicious and nutritious meals. Gardeners find a place in the medieval garden, as they can use their skills to cultivate and maintain the garden. Scholars find a place in the medieval garden, as they can study the history and culture of the garden and its plants. Culture hounds find a place in the medieval garden, as they can appreciate the art and architecture of the garden. Gourmands find a place in the medieval garden, as they can enjoy the fruits of the garden. Travelers find a place in the medieval garden, as they can visit gardens all over the world and learn about different cultures. Researchers find a place in the medieval garden, as they can study the plants and their medicinal properties. Builders find a place in the medieval garden, as they can design and construct the garden. Writers find a place in the medieval garden, as they can write about the garden and its history.

The medieval garden has had a lasting influence on modern garden design. The gardens of the Renaissance, Europe, the UK, and the US have all been influenced by medieval gardens. The Italian garden, the French formal garden, the English landscape garden, and the Spanish garden have all been influenced by medieval gardens. The medieval garden has also influenced modern cuisine.

The characteristics of medieval cuisine, such as the use of fresh, high-quality ingredients and the reliance on meat dishes, can still be seen in modern cuisine.

Medieval gardens have been a source of inspiration for literature and art, and their symbolism has been explored in various ways. The garden represents a dimension that is separate from everyday life, a human-scale space that is a place of peace and spiritual refreshment. The garden is depicted as a place of beauty, peace, and spiritual refreshment, and each element becomes a symbol that conveys a message. The walls have an initiatory and sacred connotation, and the garden becomes a borderland between two worlds, nature and culture. The garden is also a place of symbolism in literature and art, representing the power that humans have over nature.

In literature and art, the garden is depicted as a luxuriant place, sometimes surrounded by walls, filled with fountains, fruit trees, or domesticated animals. The garden is a place of beauty, peace, and spiritual refreshment, and each element becomes a symbol that conveys a message. The walls have an initiatory and sacred connotation, and the garden becomes a borderland between two worlds, nature and culture. The garden is also a place of symbolism in literature and art, representing the power that humans have over nature.

In medieval art, the garden is often depicted as a place of paradise, with numerous evergreen plants symbolizing immortality. The color green, which symbolized rebirth, life, everlasting life, nature, and spring, was also significant in medieval gardens. The beauty of the garden fills the viewers' heart with pleasure and encourages them to love more by showing gallant scenes and famous lovers, such as Tristan and Isolde or Lancelot.

In medieval literature, the garden is often used as a metaphor for the human condition, providing solace and reflection, and a source of inspiration and cultural foundation that can be shared by the world, regardless of their professions, hobbies, nationality, or religion. The garden is a place of beauty, peace, and spiritual refreshment, and each element becomes a symbol that conveys a message. The walls have an initiatory and sacred connotation, and the garden becomes a borderland between two worlds, nature and culture.

In conclusion, the medieval garden is a metaphor for the human condition, providing solace and reflection, and a source of inspiration and cultural foundation that can be shared by the world, regardless of their professions, hobbies, nationality, or religion. The medieval garden has influenced modern garden design and modern cuisine. The medieval garden provides a place for chefs, gardeners, scholars, culture hounds, gourmands, travelers, researchers, builders, and writers to find a place in the world. The medieval garden is a reflection of the human condition, combining beauty and utility, and providing a source of inspiration and cultural foundation that can be shared by the world.

XIV Further Reading

Medieval Monastery Life:
1. Southern, R. W. The Making of the Middle Ages. Yale University Press, 2013.
2. Lawrence, C. H. Medieval Monasticism: Forms of Religious Life in Western Europe in the Middle Ages. Longman, 2001.
3. Leclercq, Jean. The Love of Learning and the Desire for God: A Study of Monastic Culture. Fordham University Press, 1974.
4. Knowles, David. The Monastic Order in England: A History of its Development from the Times of St. Dunstan to the Fourth Lateran Council, 940-1216. Cambridge University Press, 1963.
5. Cistercian Studies Quarterly. Cistercian Publications, 1966.

Medieval Castle Life:
1. Johnson, Matthew. Behind the Castle Gate: From Medieval to Renaissance. Routledge, 2002.
2. Toy, Sidney. Castles: Their Construction and History. Dover Publications, 1985.
3. Thompson, M. W. The Rise of the Castle. Cambridge University Press, 1991.
4. Kaufmann, J. E., and H. W. Kaufmann. The Medieval Fortress: Castles, Forts and Walled Cities of the Middle Ages. Da Capo Press, 2004.
5. Coulson, Charles. Castles in Medieval Society: Fortresses in England, France, and Ireland in the Central Middle Ages. Oxford University Press, 2003.

Medieval Food Practices and Diet:
1. Woolgar, C. M. The Culture of Food in England, 1200-1500. Yale University Press, 2016.
2. Henisch, Bridget Ann. Fast and Feast: Food in Medieval Society. Pennsylvania State University Press, 1976.
3. Scully, Terence. The Art of Cookery in the Middle Ages. Boydell Press, 1995.
4. Albala, Ken. Eating Right in the Renaissance. University of California Press, 2002.
5. Carlin, Martha. Medieval Southwark. Hambledon Continuum, 2004.

Medieval Garden Design:
1. Harvey, John H. The Medieval Garden. Thames & Hudson, 1991.
2. Harvey, John H. Mediaeval Gardens. Batsford, 1981.
3. Harvey, John H. The Gothic World of Anne Rice. Clarendon Press, 1996.
4. Harvey, John H. The Plantagenets and Their Gardens: A Chronicle of Plants and Gardens, 1154-1485. Sutton Publishing, 1994.
5. Harvey, John H. The English Garden. Thames & Hudson, 1990.

World Garden Design:
1. Jellicoe, Geoffrey, and Susan Jellicoe. The Landscape of Man: Shaping the Environment from Prehistory to the Present Day. Thames & Hudson, 1995.

2. Turner, Tom. Garden History: Philosophy and Design, 2000 BC-2000 AD. Spon Press, 2005.
3. Brookes, John. The Book of Garden Design. Dorling Kindersley, 1991.
4. Hunt, John Dixon. The Afterlife of Gardens. Reaktion Books, 2004.
5. Clarke, Ethne. The Art of the Islamic Garden. Crowood Press, 2004.

Social and Cultural History of the Middle Ages:
1. Duby, Georges. The Three Orders: Feudal Society Imagined. University of Chicago Press, 1982.
2. Le Goff, Jacques. Medieval Civilization, 400-1500. Blackwell Publishers, 1992.
3. Power, Eileen. Medieval Women. Cambridge University Press, 1975.
4. Brown, Peter. The World of Late Antiquity: AD 150-750. W. W. Norton & Company, 1989.
5. Davis, R. H. A History of Medieval Europe: From Constantine to Saint Louis. Longman, 2005.

Food and Spice Trade and Cultivation in the Middle Ages:
1. Miller, Naomi. Spices of Life: Piquant Recipes from Africa, Asia, and Latin America for Western Kitchens. Alfred A. Knopf, 1991.
2. Collingham, Lizzie. Curry: A Tale of Cooks and Conquerors. Oxford University Press, 2006.
3. Freedman, Paul. Out of the East: Spices and the Medieval Imagination. Yale University Press, 2008.
4. Dalby, Andrew. Dangerous Tastes: The Story of Spices. University of California Press, 2000.
5. Woolgar, C. M. The Great Household in Late Medieval England. Yale University Press, 1999.

10 More to Read

1. The Taste of Conquest: The Rise and Fall of the Three Great Cities of Spice by Michael Krondl
2. Medieval and Renaissance Spice Trade 1100-1560 by Paul Freedman
3. Spice: The History of a Temptation by Jack Turner
4. Gold & Spices: The Rise of Commerce in the Middle Ages by Jean Favier
5. The Spice Route: A History by John Keay
6. The Book of Spice: From Anise to Zedoary by John O'Connell
7. The Spice Companion: A Guide to the World of Spices by Lior Lev Sercarz
8. The Medieval Kitchen: Recipes from France and Italy by Odile Redon, Françoise Sabban, and Silvano Serventi
9. The Medieval Cookbook by Maggie Black
10. The Medieval Spice Trade: A Guide to the Historical Sources by Paul Freedman

These books provide a comprehensive look at the spice trade during the Middle Ages, including its impact on commerce, politics, and culture. They also offer insights into the history of spices, their uses, and their significance in medieval society. Whether you are a history buff, a foodie, or simply interested in learning more about the spice trade, these books are sure to provide a fascinating read.

XV Places to Visit

There are several museums in the UK and Europe that have exhibits or living history sections about the Middle Ages. Here are some examples:

UK:
1. British Museum, London: The Medieval Europe gallery showcases many of the world's greatest medieval treasures, including British, European, and Byzantine objects that tell the story of a period of great change when territorial wars and political turmoil shaped the continent we know today[1].
2. National Museums Scotland, Edinburgh: The Medieval Archaeology and History section facilitates activities, access, loans, and research partnerships, producing exhibitions, books, and multi-media[2].
3. Ashmolean Museum, Oxford: This gallery displays items from the Ashmolean's English archaeological collection – one of the finest in the world[5].
4. Map of Museums in Britain: Historic UK has a map of museums in Britain, ranging from internationally famous national museums to living history museums that present everyday life in urban and rural areas during the Middle Ages[6].

Europe:
1. The Louvre, Paris: The Louvre has a collection of medieval art and artifacts, including illuminated manuscripts, sculptures, and tapestries.
2. The British Museum, London: The Europe 1400-1800 gallery showcases many of the world's greatest treasures from the Renaissance and Baroque periods, including paintings, sculptures, and decorative arts[3].
3. The National Museum of Denmark, Copenhagen: The National Museum of Denmark has a collection of medieval artifacts, including Viking weapons, jewelry, and household items.

Living History Museums:
1. Blists Hill Victorian Town, Shropshire: This living history museum recreates life in a Victorian town, including shops, homes, and factories[4].
2. Beamish Living Museum of the North, County Durham: This living history museum recreates life in a North East England town during the Industrial Revolution, including buildings, vehicles, equipment, livestock, and costumed interpreters[4].
3. Highland Folk Museum, Scottish Highlands: This living history museum recreates life in a Scottish Highland township, including homes, a schoolhouse, a church, and a working farm[4].

Overall, there are many museums and living history museums in the UK and Europe that have exhibits or living history sections about the Middle Ages, including museums with collections of medieval art and artifacts, as well as living history museums that recreate life during the Middle Ages.

XVI   Other Resources

Yes, there are museums that have food history exhibits that include medieval food ways. Here are some examples:

1. The Getty Museum, Los Angeles: The exhibition "Eat, Drink, and Be Merry: Food in the Middle Ages and Renaissance" explores the role of food in the daily life of people in the Middle Ages and Renaissance, including the social and cultural significance of food, the preparation and presentation of food, and the symbolism of food in art and literature[1].

2. British Museum, London: The exhibition "Feeding History" explores the relationship between food, power, and control through five objects from the British Museum's collection, including a Roman silver spoon, a medieval spice box, and a 19th-century sugar bowl[3].

3. National Museums Scotland, Edinburgh: The Medieval Archaeology and History section of the museum produces exhibitions, books, and multimedia on medieval foodways, including the role of food in daily life, the preparation and presentation of food, and the symbolism of food in art and literature[6].

4. "A Hermit's Cookbook: Monks, Food and Fasting in the Middle Ages" by Andrew Jotischky is a culinary history of monasticism, exploring the role of food in the daily life of monks, including the preparation and presentation of food, and the symbolism of food in art and literature[4].

5. "The Art of Cookery in the Middle Ages" by Terence Scully is an academic examination of late medieval foodways in theory and practice, including beverages, table manners, foods for the sick, international foods, and the aesthetics of food presentation[5].

Overall, there are several museums and resources that have food history exhibits that include medieval food ways, including the Getty Museum, British Museum, National Museums Scotland, and books such as "A Hermit's Cookbook" and "The Art of Cookery in the Middle Ages."

XVII

Odds and Ends
a section of Medieval Miscellany comprised of a writer's tool, listening guides and a list of Monastic Orders

A Fableist's Guide to Medieval Garden Types

Types of medieval gardens for the imaginative fiction writers out there.

1. **The Garden of Eden:** One of the most famous gardens in medieval times was the Garden of Eden, described in the Biblical book of Genesis as a terrestrial paradise.

2. **The Peasant Plot:** Medieval gardens were essentially peasant plots that were a vital source of food, the sort of food that goes into making pottage: onions, leeks, garlic, and other vegetables.

3. **Monastic Gardens:** Medieval monasteries had gardens that were planted with medicinal herbs and vegetables, as well as decorative plants like roses, lilies, and violets.

4. **The Love Garden:** The Tower of London and the Palace of Westminster possessed extensive gardens, orchards, and vineyards. London was full of orchards and gardens both for food and pleasure.

5. **The Herbalist's Garden:** Medieval herbalists had gardens that were planted with a variety of medicinal herbs, including chamomile, lavender, and sage.

6. **The Royal Garden:** Medieval kings and queens had gardens that were planted with exotic plants and herbs, including saffron, ginger, and nutmeg.

7. **The Apothecary's Garden:** Medieval apothecaries had gardens that were planted with a variety of medicinal plants, including poppies, mandrake, and henbane.

8. **The Kitchen Garden**: Medieval kitchens had gardens that were planted with a variety of vegetables, including carrots, turnips, and parsnips.

9. **The Orchard:** Medieval orchards were planted with a variety of fruit trees, including apples, pears, and cherries.

10. **The Vineyard:** Medieval vineyards were planted with a variety of grapevines, including red and white varieties.

These 10 medieval stories about gardens or foods highlight the importance of gardens and agriculture in medieval society. From the Garden of Eden to the royal gardens of kings and queens, gardens played an important role in medieval life. Medieval gardens were planted with a variety of plants, including medicinal herbs, decorative plants, and vegetables. Medieval kitchens had gardens that were planted with a variety of vegetables, and orchards and vineyards were also important sources of food. Medieval herbalists and apothecaries had gardens that were planted with a variety of medicinal plants, and vineyards were planted with a variety of grapevines.

A Medieval Music Playlist

Creating a two-hour medieval playlist involves selecting a variety of music from the medieval period, which spanned roughly from the 5th to the 15th century. Here's a curated playlist that captures the essence of medieval music:

First Hour: Instrumental and Gregorian Chant

1. "Viderunt Omnes" - Gregorian Chant
2. "Alleluia, Pascha Nostrum" - Gregorian Chant
3. "Sumer Is Icumen In" - Medieval English Round
4. "La Rotta" - Medieval Dance Music
5. "Estampie" - Medieval Dance Music
6. "In Taberna" - Carmina Burana
7. "Lamento di Tristano" - Medieval Italian Music
8. "Chominciamento di gioia" - Francesco Landini

Second Hour: Troubadours, Minstrels, and Early Polyphony

9. "Douce Dame Jolie" - Guillaume de Machaut
10. "La Quarte Estampie Royal" - Medieval Dance Music
11. "Quant je parti" - Medieval Troubadour Song
12. "Non Sofre Santa Maria" - Alfonso X of Castile
13. "Cuncti Simus Concanentes" - Cantigas de Santa Maria
14. "Dame, vostre doulz viaire" - Guillaume de Machaut
15. "Veni, veni, venias" - Carmina Burana
16. "Ave Maria... Virgo Serena" - Josquin des Prez

This playlist offers a diverse selection of medieval music, including Gregorian chant, instrumental pieces, troubadour songs, and early polyphonic compositions. It represents the rich musical heritage of the medieval period and provides a captivating journey through the sounds of the Middle Ages.

A Modern Medieval Music Playlist

Yes, there are modern musicians and groups that draw inspiration from the Troubadour tradition and create music that reflects its spirit. While the Troubadour tradition itself is medieval, its influence can still be heard in contemporary folk and world music. Here are a few examples:

1. Joan Baez: Folk singer Joan Baez has often been compared to the Troubadours due to her use of acoustic instruments and her lyrical storytelling. Her songs often carry strong messages and tell stories, much like the Troubadour tradition.

2. Donovan: The Scottish folk singer Donovan drew inspiration from the Troubadours and incorporated elements of medieval music into his songs. His 1966 album "Sunshine Superman" features tracks with a Troubadour-like quality.

3. Medieval Babes: This British musical ensemble specializes in medieval music, including Troubadour and Trouvère songs. They blend historical authenticity with modern interpretations, creating a bridge between the past and present.

4. Estampie: Estampie is a German ensemble that specializes in early music, including Troubadour and Trouvère repertoire. They use period instruments and historical research to recreate the sounds of the medieval troubadours.

5. Loreena McKennitt: Although primarily known for her Celtic-inspired music, Loreena McKennitt's compositions often carry the spirit of storytelling and balladry reminiscent of the Troubadours.

These modern musicians and groups may not strictly adhere to the Troubadour tradition, but they incorporate elements of it into their music, creating a contemporary connection to the rich heritage of Troubadour poetry and song.

Gryphon and Anonymous 4 Playlist

Creating a playlist around Gryphon and Anonymous 4 involves selecting a combination of tracks that capture the unique styles of both groups. Gryphon is known for its eclectic blend of medieval, Renaissance, and folk music with progressive rock, while Anonymous 4 is renowned for their stunning performances of medieval and Renaissance vocal music. Here's a playlist that showcases the diversity of these two ensembles:

Gryphon Tracks:

1. "Kemp's Jig" - Gryphon
2. "The Unquiet Grave" - Gryphon
3. "Juniper Suite" - Gryphon
4. "The Ploughboy's Dream" - Gryphon
5. "Midnight Mushrumps" - Gryphon
6. "The Last Flash of Gaberdine Taylor" - Gryphon
7. "Dubbel Dutch" - Gryphon

Anonymous 4 Tracks:

8. "An English Ladymass: Introit: Gaude Barbara" - Anonymous 4
9. "The Second Circle: Ave Maria" - Anonymous 4
10. "Marie et Marion: Biaute qui toutes autres pere" - Anonymous 4
11. "Miracles of Sant'Iago: Dum Pater Familias" - Anonymous 4
12. "The Lily and the Lamb: Ave Maria Gratia Plena" - Anonymous 4
13. "On Yoolis Night: Balulalow" - Anonymous 4
14. "Love's Illusion: Beata Viscera" - Anonymous 4

Collaborative Tracks:

15. "Rainbow" - Gryphon and Anonymous 4 (Collaborative Track)

This playlist provides a blend of Gryphon's instrumental pieces, which fuse various musical styles, and Anonymous 4's exquisite vocal performances of medieval and Renaissance music. The collaborative track "Rainbow" brings both ensembles together, showcasing their combined talents in a unique musical experience.

Traditional Medieval Instrument Playlist

Creating a listening list that features the cittern, mandolin, recorder, and crumhorn in early music will give you a diverse range of sounds from the medieval and Renaissance periods. Here's a selection of tracks that showcase these instruments:

Cittern:

1. "The Lady Cullen Set" - Ronn McFarlane (Cittern)
2. "Can She Excuse My Wrongs" - John Dowland (Cittern)
3. "Branle" - Pierre Attaingnant (Cittern)
4. "The Cittern" - John Renbourn (Cittern)

Mandolin:

5. "Concerto for Mandolin in C Major, RV 425" - Antonio Vivaldi (Mandolin)
6. "Mandolin Wind" - Rod Stewart (Mandolin)
7. "Allegro" from Mandolin Concerto in C Major - Wolfgang Amadeus Mozart (Mandolin)

Recorder:

8. "La Mourisque" - Tielman Susato (Recorder)
9. "Recorder Concerto in C Major, RV 443" - Antonio Vivaldi (Recorder)
10. "Greensleeves" - Traditional (Recorder)

Crumhorn:

11. "Pavane 'Mille Regretz'" - Josquin des Prez (Crumhorn)
12. "Dance of the Renaissance" - Early Music Consort of London (Crumhorn)
13. "Three Dances from Danserye" - Tielman Susato (Crumhorn)

This playlist offers a combination of classical compositions, traditional pieces, and folk-inspired tunes that highlight the unique qualities of the cittern, mandolin, recorder, and crumhorn. It provides a diverse listening experience that spans different historical periods and musical styles.

Pentangle and U.K. Folk Playlist

Creating a two-hour playlist centered around Pentangle and similar UK folk groups from the late 1960s and early 1970s will provide a rich selection of folk, folk-rock, and acoustic music. Here's a curated playlist featuring Pentangle and other artists of that era:

Pentangle:

1. "Let No Man Steal Your Thyme"
2. "Cruel Sister"
3. "Light Flight"
4. "Hunting Song"
5. "The Trees They Do Grow High"
6. "I've Got a Feeling"
7. "Train Song"
8. "Once I Had a Sweetheart"

Fairport Convention:

9. "Who Knows Where the Time Goes?" - Fairport Convention
10. "Matty Groves" - Fairport Convention
11. "She Moves Through the Fair" - Fairport Convention

Bert Jansch:

12. "Black Waterside" - Bert Jansch
13. "Needle of Death" - Bert Jansch
14. "Reynardine" - Bert Jansch

John Renbourn:

15. "Sweet Potato" - John Renbourn
16. "The Lady and the Unicorn" - John Renbourn

Steeleye Span:

17. "All Around My Hat" - Steeleye Span
18. "Thomas the Rhymer" - Steeleye Span

Sandy Denny:

19. "Fotheringay" - Sandy Denny
20. "The North Star Grassman and the Ravens" - Sandy Denny

The Incredible String Band:

21. "The Hedgehog's Song" - The Incredible String Band
22. "A Very Cellular Song" - The Incredible String Band

Nick Drake:

23. "River Man" - Nick Drake
24. "Northern Sky" - Nick Drake

This playlist encompasses a blend of folk, folk-rock, and acoustic gems from the UK folk revival era. It captures the essence of the music that Pentangle and similar groups created during that time, providing a delightful journey through the British folk scene of the late 1960s and early 1970s.

The Pentangle

The Pentangle, a British folk music ensemble formed in the late 1960s, played a pivotal role in the vibrant UK folk revival scene of that era. This remarkable quintet, consisting of Bert Jansch, John Renbourn, Jacqui McShee, Danny Thompson, and Terry Cox, transcended traditional folk boundaries by infusing their music with elements of jazz, blues, and innovative arrangements. Their eponymous debut album, "The Pentangle," captivated audiences with its virtuosic guitar work, enthralling vocal harmonies, and a repertoire that seamlessly interwove traditional folk tunes with original compositions. The Pentangle's innovative approach expanded the horizons of folk music, setting a precedent for the genre's evolution. Their influence left an indelible mark on the UK folk revival scene, helping to bridge the gap between traditional and contemporary folk and inspiring subsequent generations of folk musicians to explore new musical horizons while honoring their rich cultural heritage.

Music from the 1300s Playlist

Music from the 1300s in Europe and the UK was characterized by the transition from the Medieval to the Renaissance period. During this time, music saw significant developments in composition and style. Here's a selection of music from the 1300s in Europe and the UK:

1. "Messe de Tournai" - This is a famous example of early 14th-century European choral music. It is a Mass setting that showcases the transition from the modal system of the Middle Ages to the emerging tonal system of the Renaissance.

2. "Sumer Is Icumen In" - This is a well-known medieval English round. It's one of the earliest examples of counterpoint in English music, featuring multiple voices singing different melodies simultaneously.

3. "La Manfredina" - Composed by Francesco Landini, an Italian composer and organist of the Trecento (14th century), this piece is a beautiful example of secular music from the period.

4. "Quant je parti" - A French chanson by Guillaume de Machaut, a prominent composer of the 14th century. His compositions contributed to the development of musical notation.

5. "Sumer Is Icomen In" - A well-known English round from the 13th century, this piece reflects the joy of the summer season and features a lively and catchy melody.

6. "Agnus Dei" from the "Missa L'homme armé" - This is part of a famous Mass by Guillaume Dufay, a composer who bridged the late Medieval and early Renaissance periods.

7. "Ecco La Primavera" - Composed by Francesco Landini, this piece exemplifies the Italian Trecento style, characterized by sweet melodies and polyphonic texture.

8. "Se la face ay pale" - A song by Guillaume Dufay, this piece showcases the emerging Renaissance style with clear and expressive melodies.

These selections provide a glimpse into the musical richness of the 1300s, a period marked by both the culmination of medieval traditions and the early stirrings of the Renaissance. They showcase a variety of styles, from the more straightforward and rhythmically lively songs to the increasingly complex and harmonically rich compositions of the time.

Gregorian Chant Playlist

Listening to medieval plainsong, also known as Gregorian chant, can transport you to a world of serene spirituality and timeless beauty. Here's a selection of Gregorian chant pieces that would make for a meditative and contemplative listening experience, akin to what medieval monks might have practiced:

1. "Viderunt Omnes" - Anonymous
2. "Kyrie Eleison" - Gregorian Chant
3. "Ave Maria" - Gregorian Chant
4. "Dies Irae" - Anonymous
5. "Veni Creator Spiritus" - Gregorian Chant
6. "Salve Regina" - Gregorian Chant
7. "Pange Lingua" - Gregorian Chant
8. "Miserere Mei, Deus" - Gregorio Allegri
9. "Agnus Dei" - Gregorian Chant
10. "Te Deum" - Gregorian Chant

These chants are characterized by their simplicity, haunting melodies, and spiritual depth, making them a beautiful representation of the medieval monastic tradition. Listening to them can evoke a sense of peace and reflection reminiscent of the monastic life in the Middle Ages.

Monastic Groups that Maintained Gardens in the Middle Ages

Many monastic groups during medieval times maintained gardens as an integral part of their monastic life. These gardens served various purposes, including providing food, herbs for medicinal use, and contemplative spaces for the monks. Some of the notable monastic orders that kept gardens during the medieval period include:

1. **Benedictines:** The Benedictine monastic order, founded by St. Benedict of Nursia in the 6th century, is renowned for its dedication to manual labor and self-sufficiency. Benedictine monasteries often had extensive gardens where monks cultivated vegetables, fruits, and herbs. These gardens were used to feed the monastic community and to provide ingredients for herbal remedies.

2. **Cistercians:** The Cistercian order, an offshoot of the Benedictines, placed a strong emphasis on self-sufficiency and manual labor. Cistercian monasteries typically had well-organized gardens, orchards, and vineyards to produce food and wine. They also designed their gardens with a sense of simplicity and functionality.

3. **Carthusians**: Carthusian monasteries, known for their extreme asceticism and solitude, had gardens within their enclosed hermitages. These gardens were small, private spaces where individual monks could cultivate herbs and vegetables for their personal use.

4. **Hospitallers**: The Knights Hospitaller, a military monastic order, operated hospitals and provided care to the sick and wounded during the medieval period. Some Hospitaller establishments had gardens where medicinal herbs were grown for the treatment of patients.

5. **Trappists:** The Trappist order, a strict branch of the Cistercians, emphasized self-sufficiency and manual labor. Trappist monasteries often maintained gardens for agriculture and cultivated herbs for medicinal purposes.

6. **Dominicans and Franciscans**: While the primary focus of these mendicant orders was preaching and service to the community, some of their monasteries had gardens for the cultivation of herbs and vegetables to support their members and serve the needs of the local population.

These monastic gardens played a vital role in sustaining the monastic communities, contributing to their self-sufficiency, and providing a peaceful and contemplative environment for reflection and spiritual growth.

XVIII.

Five Medieval Prayers

In Medieval life, prayer held a paramount role, serving as the spiritual anchor that guided both the individual and the community. This profound devotion to prayer extended to the medieval garden, where faith and horticulture intertwined.

Medieval gardens were not just places of beauty; they were sanctuaries for quiet contemplation and prayer, particularly within the tranquil cloister gardens of monasteries. The carefully chosen plants and their allegorical arrangements in these gardens symbolized the divine order of the natural world, reinforcing the idea that gardening itself was an act of devotion.

Furthermore, many plants cultivated, often for medicinal purposes, were seen as conduits of God's healing power, underlining the essential role of prayer in the process of healing. These gardens were physical manifestations of the connection between the spiritual and the earthly, making prayer an integral part of both medieval life and the life of a medieval garden.

Two Monastic Prayers

During the medieval period, monastic prayers often included expressions of gratitude and contemplation, including those related to feasts and meals.

Here are two monastic prayers from the 9th to the 13th centuries that reflect the significance of feasts and communal meals in the monastic life:

Prayer of Thanks for the Feast

"Lord, as we gather at this feast, we thank You for the bounty of the table before us. Bless those who have prepared this meal with love and care. May it nourish our bodies and strengthen our spirits, that we may continue to serve You with love and devotion. In Your name, we pray. Amen."

Prayer for a Feast Day

"O God, on this holy feast day, we come together as a community to celebrate Your goodness and grace. As we share this meal, may we be reminded of the spiritual nourishment You provide for our souls. Grant us the strength and wisdom to live our lives in accordance with Your will. Bless our fellowship and deepen our sense of unity. In Your mercy, hear our prayer. Amen."

§

These prayers acknowledge the importance of communal feasts in monastic life, where monks and nuns came together to give thanks, strengthen their bonds, and find spiritual nourishment in both the physical and the divine.

Two Medieval Prayers

Medieval prayers often included expressions of gratitude for the bounty of food and the beauty of gardens. These prayers reflected the importance of sustenance and the natural world in the lives of medieval people. Here are a couple of examples:

Prayer of Thanks for Food

"O God, from whom all good things do come: Grant to us thy humble servants, that by thy holy inspiration we may think those things that be right, and by thy merciful guiding may perform the same; through our Lord Jesus Christ. Amen."

Prayer for a Bountiful Garden

"Almighty God, Lord of heaven and earth, bless this garden that it may be a source of nourishment for our bodies and a place of beauty and solace for our souls. May the seeds we have sown yield a bountiful harvest, and may your grace be upon us as we tend to this earth. In your name, we pray. Amen."

§

These prayers reflect the deep connection between spirituality and the natural world in medieval times, acknowledging the divine provision of food and the significance of gardens as places of sustenance and spiritual reflection.

Typical Closing Prayer for Medieval Services

In the Name of the Father, the Son, and the Holy Spirit, Amen.

O Lord our God,
we, your humble servants,
have gathered in your house
to worship and give thanks.

As we prepare to depart from this sacred place,
we beseech you to
grant us your blessings
and guidance.

May your grace be upon us as we go about our daily lives,
and may we carry the teachings and love we have received
here in our hearts.

Strengthen our faith, O Lord, and grant us the strength to
live according to your commandments.

Protect us from harm, both physical and spiritual, and grant
us your peace that surpasses all understanding.

In your holy name,
we pray.

Amen